Southern Living

Slow Cooker

C O O K B O O K

Oxmoor House

Southern Living
Slow Cooker
COOKBOOK

Front cover: Barbecue-Beef Sandwiches, page 10, photography by Howard L. Puckett; styling by Ashley J. Wyatt; and food styling by Jan A. Smith.
Back cover: Fudgy Caramel Pudding Cake, page 88; photography by Howard L. Puckett; styling by Ashley J. Wyatt; and food styling by Jan A. Smith

Southern Living® Slow Cooker Cookbook
©2002 by Oxmoor House, Inc.
Book Division of Southern Progress Corporation
P.O. Box 2463, Birmingham, AL 35201

Created especially for *Southern Living At HOME™*,
the Direct Selling Division of Southern Progress Corporation

For information about *Southern Living At HOME™*, please write to:
Consultant Services
P.O. Box 830951
Birmingham, AL 35283-0951

ISBN:0-8487-2647-2
Printed in the United States of America
Sixth Printing 2004

Oxmoor House, Inc.
Vice President, Editor-In-Chief: **Nancy Fitzpatrick Wyatt**
Executive Editor: **Katherine M. Eakin**
Art Director: **Cynthia R. Cooper**

Southern Living At HOME™
Vice President and Executive Director: **Dianne Mooney**
Design Editor: **Melanie Grant**

Southern Living® Slow Cooker Cookbook
Editor: **Alyson Moreland Haynes**
Art Director: **Clare T. Minges**
Copy Editor: **Jacqueline Giovanelli**
Assistant Foods Editor: **Carolyn B. Land, R.D.**
Editorial Assistants: **Jane Lorberau Gentry, Diane Rose**
Contributing Copy Editor: **Dolores Hydock**
Test Kitchens Director: **Elizabeth Tyler Luckett**
Assistant Director: **Julie Christopher** Recipe Editor: **Gayle Hays Sadler**
Test Kitchens Staff: **Jennifer Cofield; Gretchen P. Feldtman, R.D.;
David Gallent; Ana Kelly; Kathleen Royal Phillips; Jan A. Smith; Kelly Wilton (intern)**
Photographers: **Ralph Anderson, Jim Bathie, Tina Cornett, Colleen Duffley,
Brit Huckabay, Becky Luigart-Stayner, Randy Mayor, Howard L. Puckett**
Photo Stylists: **Cindy Manning Barr, Kay E. Clarke, Virginia R. Cravens, Jan Gautro,
Mary Catherine Muir, Fonda Shaia, Ashley J. Wyatt**
Production Manager: **Greg Amason**
Production Assistant: **Faye Porter Bonner**

WELCOME

The slow cooker has finally earned the respect it deserves! As you may already have discovered, it's the modern cook's most important asset. Here you'll find recipes to begin before you leave home in the morning for delicious dinners that night, along with plenty of recipes with shorter cook times. For handy reference, you'll find a clock icon beside the title of recipes that cook in six hours or less.

Your slow cooker is the most forgiving of cooking options. No basting, no eyeballing, no babysitting. But convenience is not the only benefit . . . great taste is another! And all these recipes deliver on both accounts. Besides chapters devoted to beef, poultry, pork, lamb, veal, venison, seafood, and meatless main dishes, there are also a few surprises that add to the slow cooker's culinary reputation. Some of the most highly rated items came from Extras—the chapter devoted to beverages, side dishes, snacks, desserts, and condiments. Lemon-Fig Preserves and Cranberry-Cardamom Relish received all "3s," the highest score given by our test kitchens staff. Another favorite of that chapter, Fudgy Caramel Pudding Cake, makes the perfect dessert after a little league game or a night at the movies.

Despite the universal appeal of slow cookers and the easy, hands-free meals they offer, not all slow cookers are created alike. To ensure that our recipes provide the most accurate cook times, we tested with old and new models and different sizes of cookers. Our discovery: Newer models cook hotter. Be sure to double-check the cook times depending on the age of your cooker. If the recipe calls for a 3-quart cooker and you own a 6-quart, reduce the cook time (otherwise the dish may burn). Some meat recipes call for the dish to be cooked on high heat for one hour and then reduced to low heat. This allows the slow cooker to heat up faster and the heat to penetrate the cut of meat and eradicate any bacteria. For the same reason, any piece of meat larger than a couple of pounds must be cut in half so the center will reach recommended temperatures in less time.

Here at *Southern Living At HOME,* one of our goals is to simplify day-to-day living. We hope that the mouthwatering, memory-making recipes you find here will enable you to spend more time reaping some of life's most wonderful rewards.

Alyson M. Haynes

contents

beef

Boeuf Bourguignon (Beef Burgundy)

Boeuf Bourguignon (Beef Burgundy) ⊘

Substitute 1 (16-ounce) bag frozen small whole onions, thawed and drained, for the fresh onions, if desired.

1 (10-ounce) package fresh pearl onions
1 (2-pound) top round steak
2½ cups sliced onion (1 large)
1 garlic clove, minced
Cooking spray
⅓ cup all-purpose flour
1 (10½-ounce) can condensed beef broth, undiluted
½ cup dry red wine
2 tablespoons tomato paste
½ teaspoon dried thyme
½ teaspoon salt
¼ teaspoon pepper
1 bay leaf
1 (8-ounce) package fresh mushrooms
3 cups hot cooked medium egg noodles (about 6 ounces uncooked), cooked without salt or fat
1½ teaspoons fresh thyme leaves (optional)

We tested Beef and Bean Bake with honey barbecue sauce for a slightly sweet flavor, but any thick sauce will work. Try a spicy sauce for a change of pace.

1. Drop pearl onions in boiling water, and cook 1 minute. Drain onions, and peel.

2. Trim fat from steak; cut steak into 1½-inch cubes. Place a large nonstick skillet over medium-high heat until hot. Add steak; sauté 5 minutes or until browned. Place steak in a 3-quart electric slow cooker. Add sliced onion and garlic to skillet; coat with cooking spray, and sauté over medium-high heat 5 minutes or until tender. Sprinkle flour over onion mixture, and cook 1 minute, stirring constantly. Gradually add broth, wine, and tomato paste, stirring constantly. Cook 1 minute or until thick. Add pearl onions, thyme, salt, pepper, bay leaf, and mushrooms.

3. Pour wine mixture over beef in slow cooker. Cover with lid; cook on high-heat setting 1 hour. Reduce to low-heat setting, and cook 4 to 5 hours. Discard bay leaf. Serve over noodles. Sprinkle with thyme leaves, if desired. Yield: 6 servings (serving size: 1 cup beef mixture and ½ cup noodles).

Diabetic Exchanges: 1½ Starch, 2 Veg, 5 L Meat
Per serving: CAL 411 (16% from fat); PRO 43.3g; FAT 7.3g (sat 2.3g); CARB 41.1g; FIB 3.3g; CHOL 120mg; IRON 5.9mg; SOD 464mg; CALC 48mg

Beef and Bean Bake ⊘

3 bacon slices
½ pound ground round
1 cup finely chopped onion
1 (15¼-ounce) can lima beans, drained
1 (15-ounce) can pork and beans, undrained
1 (15-ounce) can light red kidney beans, drained
½ cup ketchup
½ cup barbecue sauce
¼ cup firmly packed brown sugar
1 teaspoon dry mustard

1. Cook bacon until crisp; crumble and set aside.

2. Cook beef and onion in a large nonstick skillet over medium heat until beef is browned, stirring to crumble beef.

3. Place bacon, beef mixture, lima beans, and next 6 ingredients in a 3½-quart electric slow cooker; stir well. Cover with lid; cook on high-heat setting

1 hour. Reduce to low-heat setting, and cook 3 to 4 hours. Yield: 6 servings (serving size: 1 cup).

Diabetic Exchanges: 3 Starch, 1 Veg, 1 L Meat, ½ Fat
Per serving: CAL 301 (13% from fat); PRO 17.8g; FAT 4.4g (sat 1.3g); CARB 49.0g; FIB 9.9g; CHOL 26mg; IRON 2.8mg; SOD 928mg; CALC 65mg

Stuffed Flank Steak

1   cup herb-seasoned stuffing mix (such as Pepperidge Farm)
1   (11-ounce) can sweet whole-kernel corn, drained
½   cup coarsely shredded carrot
1   (2-pound) flank steak
Cooking spray
1   (14-ounce) jar marinara-style pasta sauce (such as Newman's Own Venetian Spaghetti Sauce)

1. Combine first 3 ingredients in a bowl; toss well, and set aside.

2. Trim fat from steak. Using a sharp knife, cut horizontally through center of steak, cutting to, but not through, other side; open flat, as you would a book. Place steak between 2 sheets of heavy-duty plastic wrap, and flatten to an even thickness using a meat mallet or rolling pin. Discard plastic wrap. Spread stuffing mixture over steak, leaving a 1-inch margin around outside edges. Roll up steak, jelly-roll fashion, starting with long side. Secure at 2-inch intervals with heavy string.

3. Place a large nonstick skillet over medium-high heat until hot. Coat steak with cooking spray, and place in skillet, browning well on all sides. Place steak in a 6-quart electric slow cooker coated with cooking spray. Pour pasta sauce over steak.

4. Cover with lid; cook on high-heat setting 1 hour. Reduce to low-heat setting, and cook 7 hours or until steak is tender. Remove steak from slow cooker; discard string. Cut steak into 8 slices; serve with sauce. Yield: 8 servings (serving size: 1 slice steak and 3½ tablespoons sauce).

Diabetic Exchanges: 1 Starch, 3 L Meat
Per serving: CAL 258 (37% from fat); PRO 25.6g; FAT 10.1g (sat 3.8g); CARB 13.5g; FIB 2.4g; CHOL 58mg; IRON 3.4mg; SOD 500mg; CALC 38mg

Rio Grande Meat Loaf ⏱

Cooking spray
1   (15-ounce) can black beans, rinsed and drained
½   cup chopped onion
½   cup chopped green bell pepper
⅓   cup chopped fresh cilantro
2   tablespoons minced seeded jalapeño pepper
1   teaspoon salt
2   teaspoons ground cumin
2   teaspoons chili powder
½   teaspoon pepper
4   taco shells, finely crushed
2   large egg whites
3   large garlic cloves, minced
2   pounds ground round
½   cup salsa

1. Coat a 3½-quart electric slow cooker with cooking spray. Tear off two sheets of aluminum foil long enough to fit in bottom of slow cooker and to extend 3 inches over each side of slow

Made with black beans, jalapeño pepper, and crushed taco shells, Rio Grande Meat Loaf brings a Mexican fiesta to your dinner table. Serve it with yellow rice and guacamole salad.

cooker. Fold each foil sheet lengthwise to form a 2-inch-wide strip. Arrange foil strips in a cross fashion in cooker, pressing strips to bottom of cooker and extending ends over sides of cooker.

2. Combine beans and next 11 ingredients in a large bowl; stir well. Crumble beef over vegetable mixture, and stir just until blended. Shape mixture into a loaf the shape of the slow cooker container. Place loaf in slow cooker over foil strips. (Foil strips become "handles" to remove meat loaf from slow cooker.)

3. Cover with lid; cook on high-heat setting 1 hour. Reduce to low-heat setting, and cook 2 to 3 hours or until done. Use foil strips to lift meat loaf from cooker. Let meat loaf stand 10 minutes before serving. Cut into wedges. Spoon 1 tablespoon salsa over each serving. Yield: 8 servings.

Diabetic Exchanges: ½ Starch, 1 Veg, 3½ L Meat
Per serving: CAL 207 (25% from fat); PRO 27.8g; FAT 5.8g (sat 1.7g); CARB 11.5g; FIB 3.3g; CHOL 60mg; IRON 3.1mg; SOD 525mg; CALC 32mg

Barbecue-Beef Sandwiches

2   (1¼-pound) flank steaks
⅓   cup dark brown sugar, divided
¾   teaspoon black pepper
1   (6-ounce) can tomato paste
1   cup chopped onion
1   cup ketchup
1   tablespoon chili powder
3   tablespoons cider vinegar
2   tablespoons Worcestershire sauce
2   tablespoons molasses
1   teaspoon salt
1   teaspoon dry mustard
2   teaspoons prepared mustard
12 (2½-ounce) sandwich buns with sesame seeds, split
24 red onion rings
36 dill pickle slices

1. Trim fat from steaks; cut each steak in half crosswise. Combine 1 tablespoon brown sugar and pepper; stir well. Rub steaks with sugar mixture. Place remaining brown sugar, tomato paste, and next 9 ingredients in a 4½-quart electric slow cooker; stir well. Add steaks, turning to coat.

Cover with lid; cook on high-heat setting 1 hour. Reduce to low-heat setting, and cook 7 to 8 hours or until steak is tender. Remove steak from slow cooker, reserving sauce in cooker.

2. Shred steak with 2 forks. Return shredded steak to cooker; stir well to coat with sauce. Spoon ½ cup steak mixture onto bottom half of each bun; top each with 2 onion rings and 3 pickle slices. Cover with tops of buns. Yield: 12 servings.

Diabetic Exchanges: 3 Starch, 2½ L Meat, ½ Fat
Per serving: CAL 375 (26% from fat); PRO 26.7g; FAT 10.8g (sat 4.2g); CARB 44.1g; FIB 2.9g; CHOL 49mg; IRON 4.2mg; SOD 928mg; CALC 78mg

Roasted Poblano and Beef Soup

6   medium poblano chiles (about 1¼ pounds)
3   garlic cloves, unpeeled
1   cup beef broth, divided
1½ pounds lean top round steak
2   (16-ounce) cans small red beans, undrained
1   (16-ounce) jar salsa (such as Herdez Salsa Casera)
1   (14.5-ounce) can no-salt-added whole tomatoes, undrained and chopped
1   cup finely chopped onion
1   cup frozen whole-kernel corn, thawed
1   tablespoon ground cumin
2   teaspoons dried oregano
2   tablespoons fresh lime juice
⅔   cup 30%-less-fat sour cream (such as Breakstone)

1. Cut chiles in half lengthwise; discard seeds and membranes. Place chile halves, skin side up, on a foil-lined baking sheet; flatten with hand. Add unpeeled garlic to baking sheet. Broil 15 minutes or until chiles are blackened. Place chiles in a zip-top plastic bag; seal. Let stand 10 minutes. Peel chiles and garlic.

2. Place half of roasted chiles, garlic, and ¼ cup beef broth in a food processor; process until smooth. Coarsely chop remaining half of chiles.

3. Trim fat from steak; cut steak into 1-inch cubes. Place pureed chile mixture, chopped chiles, remaining ¾ cup beef broth, steak, beans, salsa, tomatoes, onion, corn, cumin, and oregano in a 3½-quart electric slow cooker; stir well. Cover with lid; cook on high-heat setting 1 hour. Reduce to low-heat setting, and cook 6 hours or until steak is tender. Stir in lime juice. Top each serving with sour cream. Yield: 10 servings (serving size: 1 cup soup and 1 tablespoon sour cream).

Diabetic Exchanges: 1 Starch, 3 Veg, 2 L Meat
Per serving: CAL 235 (18% from fat); PRO 22.8g; FAT 5.0g (sat 2.3g); CARB 29.9g; FIB 8.8g; CHOL 38mg; IRON 3.8mg; SOD 653mg; CALC 92mg

Gingered Beef with Mixed Vegetables ⌄

1½ pounds lean boneless round steak
¼ cup low-salt soy sauce, divided
½ cup fresh orange juice
1½ tablespoons chopped fresh ginger
2 garlic cloves, chopped
1½ tablespoons cornstarch
2 tablespoons brown sugar
2 tablespoons hoisin sauce
1 (16-ounce) package frozen broccoli, carrots, onions, red pepper, celery, water chestnuts, and mushrooms, thawed
4½ cups hot cooked rice, cooked without salt or fat

1. Trim fat from steak; cut steak into ¼-inch strips. Place steak strips, 3 tablespoons soy sauce, and next 3 ingredients in a 4-quart electric slow cooker; stir well. Cover with lid; cook on high-heat setting 1 hour. Reduce to low-heat setting, and cook 2½ hours.

2. Combine cornstarch, brown sugar, and remaining 1 tablespoon soy sauce; stir until well blended. Add cornstarch mixture to beef mixture in slow cooker. Stir in hoisin sauce and vegetables. Cover with lid; cook on low-heat setting 40 minutes or until vegetables are crisp-tender. Serve over rice. Yield: 6 servings (serving size: ¾ cup beef mixture and ¾ cup rice).

Diabetic Exchanges: 3 Starch, 1 Veg, 3 L Meat
Per serving: CAL 384 (12% from fat); PRO 32.2g; FAT 5.0g (sat 1.5g); CARB 49.5g; FIB 2.3g; CHOL 71mg; IRON 4.3mg; SOD 569mg; CALC 39mg

Beef Stroganoff

1 (1-pound) top round steak (1 inch thick)
1 (8-ounce) package presliced fresh mushrooms
1 cup chopped onion
1 tablespoon dried parsley flakes
2 tablespoons Dijon mustard
¾ teaspoon salt
½ teaspoon dried dill
½ teaspoon pepper
3 garlic cloves, minced
⅓ cup all-purpose flour
1 cup beef broth
1 (8-ounce) container 50%-less-fat sour cream (such as Land O' Lakes)
2 cups hot cooked medium egg noodles (about 4 ounces uncooked), cooked without salt or fat

1. Trim fat from steak; cut steak diagonally across grain into ¼-inch-thick slices. Place sliced steak, mushrooms, and next 7 ingredients in a 3-quart

Frozen vegetables team with the slow cooker to make Gingered Beef with Mixed Vegetables an effortless Asian meal.

Corned Beef and Vegetables

electric slow cooker; stir well. Place flour in a small bowl; gradually add broth, stirring with a whisk until blended. Add broth mixture to slow cooker; stir well. Cover with lid; cook on high-heat setting 1 hour. Reduce to low-heat setting, and cook 7 to 8 hours or until steak is tender. Turn slow cooker off; remove lid. Let stroganoff stand 10 minutes. Stir in sour cream. Serve stroganoff over noodles. Yield: 4 servings (serving size: about 1 cup stroganoff and ½ cup noodles).

Diabetic Exchanges: 2½ Starch, 1 Veg, 4 L Meat
Per serving: CAL 404 (22% from fat); PRO 35.8g; FAT 10.1g (sat 4.6g); CARB 43.2g; FIB 2.9g; CHOL 113mg; IRON 5.5mg; SOD 946mg; CALC 123mg

Corned Beef and Vegetables

Corned beef is beef brisket that has been cured in brine for a distinct flavor. Sometimes corned beef comes with a spice packet. If not, add 1 teaspoon black peppercorns to the cooking liquid.

1 (3¾-pound) cured corned beef brisket with spice packet
20 small boiling onions (about 1 pound), peeled
10 medium carrots (about 1¾ pounds), peeled and quartered
10 small red potatoes (about 1¼ pounds)
2 bay leaves
1 (12-ounce) bottle amber beer
3 tablespoons Dijon mustard
3 tablespoons molasses
2 large garlic cloves, crushed
1 small cabbage, cut into 10 wedges (about 1½ pounds)
5 tablespoons Dijon mustard

1. Trim fat from brisket; cut brisket in half. Place onions and next 3 ingredients in a 6½-quart electric slow cooker; place brisket on top of vegetables.
2. Combine spice packet from brisket, beer, 3 tablespoons mustard, molasses, and garlic in a bowl; stir well with a whisk. Pour mixture over brisket. Cover with lid; cook on high-heat setting 1 hour. Reduce to low-heat setting, and cook 6 hours. Add cabbage; cover and cook 1 hour or until tender. Discard bay leaves.
3. Cut brisket across grain into thin slices. Serve corned beef and vegetables with 5 tablespoons mustard. Yield: 10 servings (serving size: 3 ounces brisket, 2 onions, 4 carrot pieces, 1 potato, 1 cabbage wedge, and 1½ teaspoons mustard).

Diabetic Exchanges: 1 Starch, 4 Veg, 3 M-F Meat
Per serving: CAL 391 (42% from fat); PRO 19.9g; FAT 18.4g (sat 5.6g); CARB 36.0g; FIB 5.7g; CHOL 83mg; IRON 3.8mg; SOD 671mg; CALC 107mg

Sauerbraten

The twang of white vinegar is softened by the spicy sweetness of crumbled gingersnaps in this classic German dish. Serve the tender marinated beef and sauce over spaetzle (tiny noodles or dumplings) for authenticity.

1 (3-pound) rump roast
1½ cups sliced onion
1 cup water
1 cup white vinegar
2 tablespoons salt
2 tablespoons sugar
1 lemon, sliced
10 whole cloves
6 peppercorns
3 bay leaves
15 gingersnaps, crumbled (such as Nabisco)

1. Trim fat from roast; cut roast in half crosswise. Place roast halves in a deep glass bowl. Combine onion and next 8 ingredients; stir well. Pour mixture over meat; cover and marinate in refrigerator 24 to 36 hours, turning meat occasionally.
2. Remove roast from marinade, reserving 1½ cups marinade. Discard remaining marinade. Place roast in a 6-quart electric slow cooker; pour reserved 1½ cups marinade over meat. Cover with lid; cook on high-heat setting 1 hour. Reduce to low-heat setting, and cook 7 to 8 hours or until roast is tender.
3. Remove roast from slow cooker; set aside, and keep warm. Increase to high-heat setting. Pour cooking liquid through a sieve into a bowl; discard solids. Return liquid to slow cooker. Add gingersnaps; cover and cook 12 minutes. Serve with roast. Yield: 6 servings (serving size: 3 ounces roast and ½ cup gravy).

Diabetic Exchanges: 1 Starch, 3 L Meat
Per serving: CAL 251 (32% from fat); PRO 24.3g; FAT 8.8g (sat 2.6g); CARB 17.5g; FIB 0.9g; CHOL 70mg; IRON 3.2mg; SOD 872mg; CALC 13mg

3. Remove roast halves from slow cooker, reserving jus (meat drippings) in cooker. Let roast stand 15 minutes; cut diagonally across grain into thin slices. Serve with jus and Horseradish Sauce. Yield: 12 servings (serving size: 3 ounces roast, 2½ tablespoons jus, and 4 teaspoons Horseradish Sauce).

Diabetic Exchanges: 3½ L Meat, ½ Fat
Per serving: CAL 207 (41% from fat); PRO 26.4g; FAT 9.5g (sat 3.6g); CARB 2.0g; FIB 0.2g; CHOL 81mg; IRON 2.8mg; SOD 344mg; CALC 32mg

Horseradish Sauce:
⅔   cup 30%-less-fat sour cream (such as
     Breakstone)
¼   cup light mayonnaise
2   tablespoons prepared horseradish
1   teaspoon grated lemon rind
½   teaspoon Worcestershire sauce
1   garlic clove, minced

1. Combine all ingredients in a small bowl, and stir well. Yield: 12 servings (serving size: 4 teaspoons).

A dinner of Beef with Horseradish Sauce becomes sandwiches the next day when served on French rolls with jus for dipping.

Beef with Horseradish Sauce

1   (4-pound) boneless sirloin tip roast
1   teaspoon salt
1   teaspoon garlic powder
¾   teaspoon dried oregano
½   teaspoon dried thyme
½   teaspoon pepper
Olive oil-flavored cooking spray
½   cup beef broth
Horseradish Sauce

1. Trim fat from roast; cut roast in half. Combine salt and next 4 ingredients in a small bowl; stir well. Rub mixture evenly over roast halves. Coat roast halves with cooking spray.

2. Place a large nonstick skillet over medium-high heat until hot. Add roast halves, browning well on all sides. Place roast halves in a 3½- to 4-quart electric slow cooker. Add beef broth to skillet, scraping to loosen browned bits from bottom of skillet. Pour broth mixture over roast halves in slow cooker. Cover with lid; cook on high-heat setting 1 hour. Reduce to low-heat setting, and cook 6 to 8 hours or until tender.

Country Steak with Gravy

1½ pounds boneless top round steak (½ inch
     thick)
1   (12-ounce) jar fat-free savory beef gravy
     (such as Heinz)
2   tablespoons tomato paste
½   teaspoon salt
½   teaspoon garlic powder
½   teaspoon pepper
½   teaspoon dried thyme
Cooking spray

1. Trim fat from steak; cut steak into 6 equal pieces. Combine gravy and next 5 ingredients in a small bowl; stir well. Layer gravy mixture and steak in a 4-quart electric slow cooker coated with cooking spray, beginning and ending with gravy mixture.

2. Cover with lid; cook on high-heat setting 1 hour. Reduce to low-heat setting, and cook 6 to 7 hours or until steak is tender. Yield: 6 servings (serving size: 3 ounces steak and ⅓ cup gravy).

Diabetic Exchanges: ½ Starch, 3½ L Meat
Per serving: CAL 170 (20% from fat); PRO 28.1g; FAT 3.8g (sat 1.3g); CARB 4.2g; FIB 0.3g; CHOL 65mg; IRON 2.6mg; SOD 587mg; CALC 6mg

Beefy Pasta Sauce

1½ pounds ground round
2 (15-ounce) cans tomato sauce
2 (14½-ounce) cans diced tomatoes, undrained
2 (6-ounce) cans tomato paste
1 (8-ounce) package sliced fresh mushrooms
1½ cups chopped onion
1 cup water
¾ cup chopped green bell pepper
2 tablespoons brown sugar
2 teaspoons dried basil
1 teaspoon dried oregano
¼ teaspoon salt
¼ teaspoon black pepper
⅛ teaspoon ground red pepper
2 garlic cloves, minced
1 beef-flavored bouillon cube

1. Cook meat in a large nonstick skillet over medium-high heat until browned; stir to crumble. Drain well. Place in a 5-quart electric slow cooker. Add tomato sauce and next 14 ingredients. Cover with lid; cook on high-heat setting 1 hour. Reduce to low-heat setting, and cook 6 to 7 hours. Yield: 10 servings (serving size: 1 cup).

Diabetic Exchanges: ½ Starch, 3 Veg, 2 L Meat
Per serving: CAL 183 (12% from fat); PRO 19.4g; FAT 2.7g (sat 1.0g); CARB 23.3g; FIB 4.6g; CHOL 36mg; IRON 3.3mg; SOD 818mg; CALC 43mg

Peppered Beef Brisket in Beer

1 (4-pound) beef brisket
1 large onion (about 8 ounces), sliced and separated into rings
¾ teaspoon pepper
3 tablespoons all-purpose flour
3 tablespoons brown sugar
2 garlic cloves, minced
¾ cup beer
½ cup chili sauce

1. Trim fat from brisket; cut brisket in half. Place onion rings in a 4-quart electric slow cooker. Sprinkle pepper evenly over brisket halves. Place brisket halves over onion rings in slow cooker. Place flour, brown sugar, and garlic in a small

Spoon Beefy Pasta Sauce over cheese ravioli, tortellini, or spaghetti, and top with sliced fresh basil for a meal the whole family will love.

bowl; gradually add beer and chili sauce, stirring until well blended. Pour flour mixture over brisket. Cover with lid; cook on high-heat setting 1 hour. Reduce to low-heat setting, and cook 6 to 8 hours or until tender. Slice brisket, and serve with sauce. Yield: 12 servings (serving size: 3 ounces brisket and about 6 tablespoons sauce).

Diabetic Exchanges: 1 Starch, 3 L Meat
Per serving: CAL 250 (40% from fat); PRO 25.8g; FAT 10.9g (sat 3.9g); CARB 10.6g; FIB 0.4g; CHOL 79mg; IRON 2.6mg; SOD 383mg; CALC 14mg

Homestyle Chili

¾ pound beef stew meat, cut into ½-inch pieces
2 (16-ounce) cans chili beans in mild sauce (such as Bush's), undrained
1 (14½-ounce) can stewed tomatoes, drained
1 (10-ounce) package frozen chopped green bell pepper (about 3 cups)
1 cup frozen chopped onion
1 tablespoon salt-free Mexican seasoning (such as Spice Hunter)
8 tablespoons 30%-less-fat sour cream (such as Breakstone)
8 teaspoons chopped fresh cilantro

1. Place first 6 ingredients in a 6-quart electric slow cooker; stir well. Cover with lid; cook on high-heat setting 1 hour. Reduce to low-heat setting, and cook 7 hours.

2. Ladle chili into bowls; top with sour cream and cilantro. Yield: 8 servings (serving size: 1 cup chili, 1 tablespoon sour cream, and 1 teaspoon cilantro).

Diabetic Exchanges: 1½ Starch, 1 Veg, 1 M-F Meat
Per serving: CAL 222 (30% from fat); PRO 14.9g; FAT 7.5g (sat 3.2g); CARB 25.1g; FIB 6.7g; CHOL 39mg; IRON 2.6mg; SOD 553mg; CALC 93mg

Hungarian Goulash

2 pounds round steak (¾ inch thick)
1 cup chopped onion
Olive oil-flavored cooking spray
1 garlic clove, minced
2 tablespoons all-purpose flour
1 tablespoon paprika
1 teaspoon salt
½ teaspoon pepper
¼ teaspoon dried thyme
1 (28-ounce) can whole tomatoes, undrained and chopped
1 bay leaf
1 (8-ounce) carton 30%-less-fat sour cream (such as Breakstone)
8 cups hot cooked medium egg noodles (about 1 pound uncooked), cooked without salt or fat

1. Trim fat from steak; cut steak into ½-inch cubes. Place a large nonstick skillet over medium-high heat until hot. Add steak and onion. Coat steak and onion with cooking spray; sauté until steak is browned and onions are tender. Add garlic, and sauté 30 seconds.

2. Combine flour and next 4 ingredients in a small bowl; stir well. Add flour mixture to steak mixture, tossing well to coat. Add tomatoes and bay leaf; stir well. Place steak mixture in a 3½-quart electric slow cooker. Cover with lid; cook on high-heat setting 1 hour. Reduce to low-heat setting, and cook 5 to 6 hours. Stir in sour cream; discard bay leaf. Serve over noodles. Yield: 8 servings (serving size: ¾ cup goulash and 1 cup noodles).

Diabetic Exchanges: 3 Starch, 1 Veg, 4 L Meat
Per serving: CAL 463 (20% from fat); PRO 41.1g; FAT 10.3g (sat 4.1g); CARB 49.8g; FIB 3.5g; CHOL 144mg; IRON 6.2mg; SOD 505mg; CALC 106mg

Since Homestyle Chili uses staple ingredients, throw this dish together in the morning for a warm supper on a cold night.

Picadillo 🕐

In Cuba, picadillo is served with rice and black beans; in Mexico it's used as a stuffing and served with tortillas.

2   pounds ground round
1½ cups chopped green bell pepper
1   cup chopped onion
1   cup sliced green onions
4   garlic cloves, minced
1   (14½-ounce) can diced tomatoes, undrained
1   (8-ounce) can tomato sauce
⅓   cup chopped pitted dates
⅓   cup chopped dried apricots
¼   cup sliced pimiento-stuffed olives
1   tablespoon ground cumin
1   teaspoon ground cinnamon
½   teaspoon salt
½   teaspoon dried oregano
¼   teaspoon ground red pepper
¼   teaspoon pepper
¼   cup slivered almonds, toasted
28 (6-inch) flour tortillas

1. Cook meat, bell pepper, onions, and garlic in a large nonstick skillet over medium-high heat until meat is browned, stirring to crumble meat. Drain well.

2. Place meat mixture in a 4-quart electric slow cooker. Add diced tomatoes and next 10 ingredients; stir well. Cover with lid; cook on high-heat setting 3 hours. Stir in almonds. Serve with tortillas. Yield: 14 servings (serving size: ½ cup picadillo and 2 tortillas).

Diabetic Exchanges: 2 Starch, 1 Veg, ½ Fruit, 2 L Meat, ½ Fat
Per serving: CAL 329 (23% from fat); PRO 20.8g; FAT 8.3g (sat 2.5g); CARB 43.2g; FIB 4.6g; CHOL 24mg; IRON 4.4mg; SOD 761mg; CALC 72mg

Company Pot Roast

Morels impart a smoky, earthy flavor to this dish, but you may substitute dried shiitake mushrooms, if desired.

2   pounds lean chuck roast
¼   cup low-salt soy sauce
2   garlic cloves, minced
1   cup beef broth
1   (.35-ounce) package dried morel mushrooms
1   tablespoon cracked black pepper
3   tablespoons sun-dried tomato paste
2   medium onions (about ¾ pound), quartered

1   (16-ounce) package carrots, peeled and cut into 2-inch pieces
16 small round red potatoes (about 2 pounds), halved
1   tablespoon vegetable oil
1½ tablespoons all-purpose flour
3   tablespoons water

1. Trim fat from roast. Combine roast, soy sauce, and garlic in a large zip-top plastic bag; seal bag, and marinate in refrigerator at least 8 hours, turning bag occasionally.

2. Bring broth to a boil in a small saucepan; add mushrooms. Remove from heat; cover, and let stand 20 minutes. Drain mushrooms through a coffee filter-lined sieve or cheesecloth-lined colander, reserving broth mixture.

3. Remove roast from bag, reserving marinade. Sprinkle roast with pepper, gently pressing pepper into roast. Combine reserved marinade, mushroom broth mixture, and tomato paste; stir well, and set aside.

Picadillo blends ground meat with tomatoes, olives, almonds, sweet spices, and, traditionally, raisins. We replaced the raisins with dates and dried apricots for a flavor twist.

Pumpernickel Roast

4. Place mushrooms, onion, carrot, and potato in a 6-quart electric slow cooker; toss gently.

5. Heat oil in a large skillet over medium-high heat. Add roast, browning well on all sides. Place roast over vegetables in slow cooker. Pour tomato paste mixture into skillet, scraping bottom of skillet to remove browned bits. Pour tomato paste mixture over roast and vegetables. Cover with lid; cook on high-heat setting 1 hour. Reduce to low-heat setting, and cook 8 hours or until roast is tender. Place roast and vegetables on a serving platter; keep warm. Reserve liquid in slow cooker; increase to high-heat setting.

6. Place flour in a small bowl. Gradually add water, stirring with a whisk until well blended. Add flour mixture to liquid in slow cooker. Cook, uncovered, 15 minutes or until gravy is slightly thick, stirring frequently. Serve gravy with sliced pot roast and vegetables. Yield: 8 servings (serving size: 3 ounces roast, 1 onion wedge, about 3 carrot pieces, 4 potato halves, and about ¼ cup gravy).

Diabetic Exchanges: 2 Starch, 2 Veg, 2½ L Meat, 1 Fat
Per serving: CAL 384 (29% from fat); PRO 27.4g; FAT 12.5g (sat 4.2g); CARB 40.0g; FIB 5.6g; CHOL 75.7mg; IRON 5.0mg; SOD 488mg; CALC 49mg

Pumpernickel Roast

1   (10-ounce) package fresh pearl onions
1   (3½-pound) sirloin tip roast
Cooking spray
1   (12-ounce) bottle stout beer (such as Samuel
    Adams Cream Stout)
¼   cup stone-ground mustard
1   tablespoon caraway seeds
1½ teaspoons salt
1   teaspoon pepper
⅓   cup all-purpose flour
4   cups hot cooked medium egg noodles (about 8
    ounces uncooked), cooked without salt or fat

1. Drop pearl onions in boiling water, and cook 1 minute. Drain onions, and peel.

2. Trim fat from roast; cut roast in half. Coat roast halves with cooking spray. Place a large nonstick skillet over medium-high heat until hot. Add roast halves, browning well on all sides.

3. Place onions in a 4-quart electric slow cooker; place roast halves on top of onions. Combine beer and next 4 ingredients; stir well, and pour over roast. Cover with lid; cook on high-heat setting 1 hour. Reduce to low-heat setting, and cook 8 to 10 hours or until roast is tender. Remove roast halves and onions from slow cooker; keep warm. Reserve liquid in cooker. Increase to high-heat setting.

4. Place flour in a small bowl. Gradually add ½ cup reserved cooking liquid to flour, stirring with a whisk until well blended. Stir flour mixture into remaining liquid in slow cooker; cook, uncovered, 15 minutes or until thick, stirring frequently. Slice roast. Serve roast and onions over noodles; top with gravy. Yield: 8 servings (serving size: ½ cup noodles, 4 ounces roast, 2 tablespoons onions, and ½ cup gravy).

Diabetic Exchanges: 2 Starch, 1 Veg, 4 L Meat
Per serving: CAL 385 (22% from fat); PRO 38.2g; FAT 9.3g (sat 3.0g); CARB 33.1g; FIB 2.5g; CHOL 118mg; IRON 5.3mg; SOD 642mg; CALC 41mg

Mediterranean Beef Soup

2   medium zucchini (about 1¼ pounds), cut
     into bite-size pieces
1   large onion, cut into 6 wedges
1   (2-inch) cinnamon stick
¾   pound beef stew meat, cut into ½-inch cubes
2   (14.5-ounce) cans diced tomatoes with basil,
     garlic, and oregano, undrained
½   teaspoon pepper
Cooking spray
3½   cups hot cooked orzo (about 1¾ cups
     uncooked rice-shaped pasta), cooked
     without salt or fat

1. Place first 6 ingredients in a 3½-quart electric slow cooker coated with cooking spray; stir well. Cover with lid; cook on high-heat setting 1 hour. Reduce to low-heat setting, and cook 7 to 9 hours. Discard cinnamon stick. Serve over cooked orzo. Yield: 7 servings (serving size: 1 cup soup and ½ cup pasta).

Diabetic Exchanges: 2 Starch, 3 Veg, 1 L Meat
Per serving: CAL 304 (12% from fat); PRO 17.6g; FAT 4.2g (sat 1.4g); CARB 48.7g; FIB 3.2g; CHOL 30mg; IRON 4.8mg; SOD 631mg; CALC 99mg

poultry

Provençale Chicken Supper

Garlic-Rosemary Chicken

Provençale Chicken Supper ⊘

4   (6-ounce) skinless, bone-in chicken breast halves
2   teaspoons dried basil
¼   teaspoon salt, divided
¼   teaspoon black pepper, divided
1   cup diced yellow bell pepper
1   (16-ounce) can navy beans, rinsed and drained
1   (14½-ounce) can pasta-style chunky tomatoes, undrained
Basil leaves (optional)

1. Place chicken in a 4½-quart electric slow cooker; sprinkle with basil, ⅛ teaspoon salt, and ⅛ teaspoon black pepper.

2. Combine remaining ⅛ teaspoon salt, remaining ⅛ teaspoon black pepper, bell pepper, beans, and tomatoes in a bowl; stir well. Spoon over chicken. Cover with lid; cook on high-heat setting 1 hour. Reduce to low-heat setting, and cook 5 hours. Spoon bean mixture into each of 4 shallow bowls; top each with 1 chicken breast half. Garnish with basil leaves, if desired. Yield: 4 servings (serving size: 1 chicken breast half and about ¾ cup bean mixture).

Diabetic Exchanges: 1 Starch, 2 Veg, 3½ V-L Meat
Per serving: CAL 238 (7% from fat); PRO 31.6g; FAT 1.7g (sat 0.5g); CARB 24.2g; FIB 5.3g; CHOL 63mg; IRON 3.1mg; SOD 555mg; CALC 92mg

Garlic-Rosemary Chicken

1   (5-pound) roasting chicken, skinned
2   (5-inch) rosemary sprigs
2   celery stalks with leaves, each cut into 4 pieces
2   small onions, quartered
16 garlic cloves
1   tablespoon lemon juice
½   teaspoon salt
½   teaspoon pepper
½   teaspoon paprika
Rosemary sprigs (optional)
1   lemon, halved (optional)

1. Remove and discard giblets and neck from chicken. Rinse chicken under cold water; pat dry. Trim excess fat. Place 2 rosemary sprigs, celery, 4 onion wedges, and 4 garlic cloves in cavity

of chicken, and tie legs together with twine. Place chicken, breast side up, in a 4-quart electric slow cooker; add remaining onion and garlic to cooker. Drizzle lemon juice over chicken; sprinkle with next 3 ingredients. Cover with lid; cook on high-heat setting 1 hour. Reduce to low-heat setting, and cook 6 hours or until chicken is tender. Discard rosemary. Serve chicken with vegetables and garlic. Garnish with additional rosemary sprigs and lemon halves, if desired. Yield: 8 servings (serving size: 3 ounces chicken, 2 garlic cloves, 1 celery piece, and 1 onion wedge).

Diabetic Exchanges: 1 Veg, 3 L Meat
Per serving: CAL 181 (33% from fat); PRO 25.4g; FAT 6.4g (sat 1.8g); CARB 4.5g; FIB 0.7g; CHOL 76mg; IRON 1.3mg; SOD 233mg; CALC 33mg

Braised Turkey Thighs with Rosemary and Potatoes ⊘

2   turkey thighs (about 1¾ pounds), skinned
¾   teaspoon salt, divided
½   teaspoon pepper, divided
Olive oil-flavored cooking spray
1   medium onion, halved lengthwise and sliced (about 1 cup)
4   cups sliced peeled baking potato (about 1½ pounds)
⅔   cup fat-free, less-sodium chicken broth
1½ teaspoons fresh or ½ teaspoon dried rosemary
4   garlic cloves, minced

1. Sprinkle thighs with ¼ teaspoon salt and ¼ teaspoon pepper. Coat a large nonstick skillet with cooking spray; place over medium-high heat until hot. Add thighs; cook 3½ minutes on each side or until browned.

2. Place onion in a 4-quart electric slow cooker; top with potato. Arrange thighs on top of potato. Combine remaining ½ teaspoon salt, remaining ¼ teaspoon pepper, broth, rosemary, and garlic; stir well. Pour broth mixture over thighs. Cover with lid; cook on high-heat setting 1 hour. Reduce to low-heat setting, and cook 5 to 6 hours or until turkey and vegetables are tender. Remove turkey from bone; discard bone. Yield: 4 servings

2. Remove carrot, chicken, and garlic from slow cooker with a slotted spoon; keep warm. Reserve cooking liquid in cooker. Increase to high-heat setting.

3. Combine cornstarch and water; stir until well blended. Stir cornstarch mixture into cooking liquid. Cook 15 minutes or until thick, stirring frequently. Place ⅓ cup carrot, 3 garlic cloves, and 2 chicken thighs on each of 4 plates. Spoon cooking liquid evenly over each serving. Yield: 4 servings.

Diabetic Exchanges: ½ Starch, 1 Veg, 4 L Meat
Per serving: CAL 236 (24% from fat); PRO 31.1g; FAT 6.1g (sat 1.5g); CARB 12.7g; FIB 2.1g; CHOL 126mg; IRON 2.4mg; SOD 589mg; CALC 53mg

Green Chile Chicken

Cooking spray
6 (4-ounce) skinless, boneless chicken breast halves
1½ cups chopped onion
1 (10¾-ounce) can condensed reduced-fat, reduced-sodium cream of chicken soup, undiluted
1 (4.5-ounce) can chopped green chiles, undrained
1 tablespoon vegetable oil
1 cup uncooked long-grain rice
2 cups water
1 teaspoon salt

1. Coat a large nonstick skillet with cooking spray; place over medium-high heat until hot. Add chicken; cook 3 minutes on each side or until browned. Remove chicken from skillet; set aside. Recoat skillet with cooking spray. Add onion; sauté until tender.

2. Place chicken in a 4- to 5-quart electric slow cooker. Combine onion, soup, and chiles; stir well. Pour over chicken. Cover with lid; cook on high-heat setting 1 hour. Reduce to low-heat setting, and cook 6 hours.

3. Heat oil in a medium saucepan over medium-high heat. Add rice; sauté 2 minutes or until rice is lightly browned. Gradually add water and salt; bring to a boil. Cover, reduce heat, and simmer

---

A few minutes of morning preparation turn Chicken and Carrots with Wine Sauce into a flavor-packed dinner.

(serving size: 3 ounces turkey, 1¼ cups potato-onion mixture, and about ¼ cup sauce).

Diabetic Exchanges: 2 Starch, 3½ L Meat
Per serving: CAL 293 (14% from fat); PRO 32.1g; FAT 4.5g (sat 1.5g); CARB 30.2g; FIB 2.5g; CHOL 111mg; IRON 3.0mg; SOD 625mg; CALC 46mg

Chicken and Carrots with Wine Sauce

Hours of cooking mellow the garlic. Serve French bread to sop up the sauce or serve over rice.
2 cups diagonally sliced carrot (about 8 ounces)
8 chicken thighs (about 2½ pounds), skinned
12 garlic cloves, peeled
½ cup dry white wine
1 teaspoon dried thyme
¾ teaspoon salt
¼ teaspoon pepper
2 tablespoons cornstarch
2 tablespoons water

1. Combine carrot, chicken, and garlic in a 4-quart electric slow cooker. Pour wine over mixture. Sprinkle with thyme, salt, and pepper. Cover with lid; cook on high-heat setting 1 hour. Reduce to low-heat setting, and cook 6 hours.

20 minutes or until liquid is absorbed and rice is tender. Serve chicken and sauce over rice. Yield: 6 servings (serving size: 1 chicken breast, ⅓ cup sauce, and ½ cup rice).

Diabetic Exchanges: 2 Starch, 1 Veg, 3 V-L Meat
Per serving: CAL 321 (14% from fat); PRO 30.1g; FAT 4.9g (sat 1.0g); CARB 36.1g; FIB 1.5g; CHOL 70mg; IRON 2.3mg; SOD 744mg; CALC 38mg

Apricot-Glazed Turkey and Sweet Potatoes

6 cups (1-inch) cubed peeled sweet potatoes (about 1¾ pounds)
1 cup apricot preserves, divided
½ teaspoon salt, divided
2 bay leaves
2 (¾-pound) turkey tenderloins

1. Place sweet potatoes, ½ cup preserves, and ¼ teaspoon salt in a 4½- to 5-quart electric slow cooker; toss well. Add bay leaves. Arrange tenderloins over sweet potatoes, and sprinkle with remaining ¼ teaspoon salt. Spread remaining ½ cup preserves over tenderloins. Cover with lid; cook on high-heat setting 1 hour. Reduce to low-heat setting, and cook 7 hours or until turkey and sweet potatoes are tender. Remove tenderloins from slow cooker, and slice. Discard bay leaves. Serve turkey with sweet potatoes and cooking liquid. Yield: 6 servings (serving size: 3 ounces turkey, ⅔ cup sweet potatoes, and ¼ cup cooking liquid).

Diabetic Exchanges: 4 Starch, 3 V-L Meat
Per serving: CAL 357 (3% from fat); PRO 31.5g; FAT 1.1g (sat 0.3g); CARB 56.2g; FIB 2.3g; CHOL 82mg; IRON 2.3mg; SOD 278mg; CALC 42mg

Spicy Chicken and Sausage Soup

1¼ cups sliced low-fat smoked sausage (about 4 ounces)
1 pound skinless, boneless chicken breast halves, cut into 1-inch pieces
3 garlic cloves, minced
1 (16-ounce) package frozen vegetable gumbo mix (such as McKenzie's)
1 (14½-ounce) can Cajun-style stewed tomatoes, undrained and chopped
1 (14½-ounce) can fat-free, less-sodium chicken broth
2 teaspoons Cajun seasoning
2 teaspoons Worcestershire sauce
½ teaspoon dried thyme
2 bay leaves
2 cups cooked long-grain rice, cooked without salt or fat
1 teaspoon hot sauce

1. Place a large nonstick skillet over medium-high heat until hot. Add sausage, chicken, and garlic; sauté 3 minutes or until chicken and sausage are browned. Place mixture in a 3½-quart electric slow cooker. Add frozen gumbo mix and next 6 ingredients; stir well.

2. Cover with lid; cook on high-heat setting 1 hour. Reduce to low-heat setting, and cook 5 hours. Stir in rice and hot sauce. Cover and cook 30 minutes. Discard bay leaves. Yield: 6 servings (serving size: 1⅓ cups).

Diabetic Exchanges: 1½ Starch, 2 Veg, 2 V-L Meat
Per serving: CAL 253 (7% from fat); PRO 25.4g; FAT 2.0g (sat 0.5g); CARB 33.5g; FIB 4.5g; CHOL 51mg; IRON 2.5mg; SOD 876mg; CALC 56mg

Serve Apricot-Glazed Turkey and Sweet Potatoes with green beans, wheat rolls, and baked apples for an ideal autumn meal.

Chicken Brunswick Stew

Be sure to use the hot pepper sauce that contains whole peppers packed in vinegar rather than the red-colored hot sauce.

5   cups chopped onion
6   (4-ounce) skinless, boneless chicken breast halves
2   (14¾-ounce) cans no-salt-added cream-style corn
2   (14½-ounce) cans no-salt-added diced tomatoes, undrained
1   (14¼-ounce) can no-salt-added chicken broth
1   (12-ounce) bottle chili sauce
¼   cup butter or stick margarine, cut into small pieces
2   tablespoons Worcestershire sauce
2   tablespoons cider vinegar
2   teaspoons dry mustard
½   teaspoon freshly ground pepper
½   teaspoon hot pepper sauce
Freshly ground pepper (optional)

1. Place onion in a 4- to 6-quart electric slow cooker; top with chicken. Add corn, tomatoes, broth, chili sauce, butter, Worcestershire sauce, vinegar, mustard, pepper, and pepper sauce; stir well. Cover with lid; cook on high-heat setting 1 hour. Reduce to low-heat setting, and cook 6 hours or until chicken is tender. Remove chicken; shred and return to stew. Ladle stew into bowls; sprinkle with additional pepper, if desired. Yield: 9 servings (serving size: 1½ cups).

Diabetic Exchanges: 2½ Starch, 1 Veg, 2 V-L Meat, 1 Fat
Per serving: CAL 302 (22% from fat); PRO 21.6g; FAT 7.5g (sat 3.6g); CARB 38.8g; FIB 4.6g; CHOL 58mg; IRON 1.6mg; SOD 1,216mg; CALC 51mg

Chill-Breaker Turkey Chili

The mild flavors in this low-fat chili make it suitable for even the youngest family member. If you prefer more heat, serve with sliced jalapeños.

1   pound fresh ground turkey (light and dark meat)
1   cup chopped onion
1   cup water
1   (30-ounce) can chili beans, undrained
1   (8-ounce) can no-salt-added tomato sauce
1   (1.25-ounce) package mild chili seasoning mix

1. Cook turkey and onion in a large nonstick skillet over medium-high heat until turkey is browned, stirring to crumble turkey.

2. Place turkey mixture in a 3½-quart electric slow cooker. Add water and remaining ingredients; stir well. Cover with lid; cook on high-heat setting 1 hour. Reduce to low-heat setting, and cook 6 to 8 hours. Yield: 5 servings (serving size: 1 cup).

Diabetic Exchanges: 3 Starch, 4 L Meat
Per serving: CAL 345 (13% from fat); PRO 37.4g; FAT 5.3g (sat 1.9g); CARB 42.4g; FIB 10.5g; CHOL 76mg; IRON 4.5mg; SOD 993mg; CALC 107mg

Lemon Pepper Turkey Breast

This slow cooker recipe yields a moist turkey breast with gravy; leftovers make delicious sandwiches. For convenience, have the butcher cut the turkey breast in half to ensure even cooking.

1   (5-pound) bone-in turkey breast, skinned and cut in half
2   teaspoons lemon pepper
2   tablespoons all-purpose flour
3   tablespoons water

1. Sprinkle turkey evenly with lemon pepper. Place turkey breast halves, meaty side down, in a 5- to 6½-quart electric slow cooker. Cover with lid; cook on high-heat setting 1 hour. Reduce to low-heat setting, and cook 7 hours or until turkey is tender. Remove turkey to a platter, reserving cooking liquid in slow cooker. Set turkey aside; keep warm.

2. Combine flour and water in a medium saucepan, stirring with a whisk until well blended. Gradually add reserved cooking liquid, stirring constantly. Bring to a boil over medium-high heat, stirring constantly. Reduce heat, and simmer 4 minutes or until thick, stirring occasionally. Serve turkey with gravy. Yield: 11 servings (serving size: 3 ounces turkey and about 2 tablespoons gravy).

Diabetic Exchanges: 3½ V-L Meat
Per serving: CAL 120 (5% from fat); PRO 25.7g; FAT 0.7g (sat 0.2g); CARB 1.2g; FIB 0.1g; CHOL 71mg; IRON 1.4mg; SOD 128mg; CALC 11mg

Chicken Brunswick Stew

Cornish Hens with Wild Mushrooms and Fresh Vegetables ⊘

2   (1½-pound) Cornish hens
½   teaspoon salt, divided
1   (14½-ounce) can fat-free, less-sodium chicken broth, divided
1   (½-ounce) package dried chanterelle mushrooms, coarsely chopped
1   tablespoon sun-dried tomato oil (reserved from tomatoes), divided
1   small onion, cut into 1-inch pieces (about ¾ cup)
¾   cup baby carrots, halved lengthwise
1   (8-ounce) package fresh cremini mushrooms, quartered
1   cup (2-inch) sliced fresh green beans
½   cup all-purpose flour
½   cup dry white wine
2   teaspoons chopped fresh or dried rosemary
6   drained oil-packed sun-dried tomato halves

Cornish Hens with Wild Mushrooms and Fresh Vegetables is a new, upscale twist for slow cooker fare.

1. Remove and discard giblets and necks from hens. Rinse hens under cold water; pat dry. Remove skin; trim excess fat. Split hens in half lengthwise. Sprinkle with ¼ teaspoon salt; set aside.

2. Bring ¾ cup chicken broth and dried mushrooms to a boil in a small saucepan. Remove from heat; cover and let stand 5 minutes. Drain, reserving mushrooms and mushroom liquid. Set both aside.

3. Heat 1 teaspoon sun-dried tomato oil in a large nonstick skillet over medium-high heat. Add onion and carrots; sauté 5 minutes. Add fresh mushrooms and green beans; sauté 3 minutes. Place vegetable mixture in a 4-quart electric slow cooker; set aside.

4. Add 2 teaspoons sun-dried tomato oil to skillet; place over medium-high heat. Place hen halves in skillet, meaty side down, and cook 4 minutes on each side or until lightly browned. Place hen halves over vegetables in slow cooker, reserving drippings in skillet.

5. Place flour in skillet. Gradually add reserved mushroom liquid, remaining broth, and wine, stirring constantly until well blended. Stir in remaining ¼ teaspoon salt and rosemary. Place over medium-high heat, and cook 4 minutes or until very thick, stirring constantly. Remove from heat; stir in reserved chanterelle mushrooms and sun-dried tomato halves. Pour mushroom mixture over hen halves. Cover with lid; cook on high-heat setting 1 hour. Reduce to low-heat setting, and cook 2 hours or until hens are tender. Yield: 4 servings (serving size: 1 Cornish hen half and about 1 cup sauce).

Diabetic Exchanges: 1 Starch, 2 Veg, 5 V-L Meat, ½ Fat
Per serving: CAL 351 (22% from fat); PRO 42.9g; FAT 8.6g (sat 1.8g); CARB 23.6g; FIB 5.1g; CHOL 114mg; IRON 4.2mg; SOD 616mg; CALC 78mg

Chicken Barbecue ⊘

1½ cups sliced onion
½   lemon, sliced and seeded
6   (6-ounce) skinless, bone-in chicken breast halves
1   (18-ounce) bottle thick and spicy original barbecue sauce
½   cup cola
¼   cup all-purpose flour
¼   cup water

1. Place onion and lemon in a 4-quart electric slow cooker; top with chicken. Combine barbecue sauce and cola; stir well. Pour over chicken. Cover with lid; cook on high-heat setting 1 hour. Reduce to low-heat setting, and cook 5 hours or until chicken is tender. Remove chicken and lemon slices from slow cooker with a slotted spoon, reserving cooking liquid in slow cooker. Set chicken aside; keep warm. Discard lemon slices. Increase to high-heat setting.

2. Place flour in a small bowl; gradually add water, stirring with a whisk until well blended. Stir flour mixture into sauce in slow cooker. Cook 10 minutes or until thick, stirring occasionally. Serve sauce over chicken. Yield: 6 servings (serving size: 1 breast half and ⅔ cup sauce).

Diabetic Exchanges: 1½ Starch, 3½ V-L Meat
Per serving: CAL 226 (12% from fat); PRO 28.6g; FAT 3.0g (sat 0.6g); CARB 19.6g; FIB 1.7g; CHOL 66mg; IRON 1.9mg; SOD 769mg; CALC 36mg

Saucy Drumsticks and Thighs ⊙

After simmering in a well-seasoned sauce, this chicken is fall-off-the-bone tender. Serve chicken and sauce over rice or egg noodles.

6   chicken drumsticks (about 1½ pounds), skinned
6   chicken thighs (about 1½ pounds), skinned
1   (14½-ounce) can diced tomatoes with roasted garlic, undrained
1   (6-ounce) can tomato paste
¼   cup dried onion flakes
2   teaspoons chicken-flavored bouillon granules
1   teaspoon dried Italian seasoning
½   teaspoon garlic powder
½   teaspoon crushed red pepper

1. Place chicken in a 4-quart electric slow cooker. Combine tomatoes and remaining ingredients; stir well. Pour over chicken. Cover with lid; cook on high-heat setting 1 hour. Reduce to low-heat setting, and cook 4 to 5 hours or until chicken is tender. Yield: 6 servings (serving size: 1 drumstick, 1 thigh, and ¾ cup sauce).

Diabetic Exchanges: 2 Veg, 4 L Meat
Per serving: CAL 232 (21% from fat); PRO 31.0g; FAT 5.3g (sat 1.3g); CARB 13.5g; FIB 1.8g; CHOL 114mg; IRON 2.7mg; SOD 762mg; CALC 59mg

Duck Breast with Fennel-Fig Sauce ⊙

The flavor of the sauce depends on the port. A high-quality port produces a better tasting sauce.

1½ cups thinly sliced fennel bulb
1   cup dried Calimyrna figs (about 8), cut in half
¾   cup sliced leek
4   (4-ounce) skinless, boneless fresh or frozen duck breast halves, thawed
½   teaspoon freshly ground pepper
⅛   teaspoon salt
½   cup port or other sweet red wine, divided
⅓   cup duck sauce (such as Kame)
2   tablespoons low-sodium soy sauce
1   tablespoon cornstarch
1   tablespoon tomato paste

1. Place first 3 ingredients in a 4-quart electric slow cooker, and stir well. Place duck breast halves over vegetables and figs; sprinkle with pepper and salt.

2. Combine ¼ cup port, duck sauce, and soy sauce in a small bowl; stir well. Pour over duck. Cover with lid; cook on high-heat setting 1 hour. Reduce to low-heat setting, and cook 2 hours or

Served with couscous, Duck Breast with Fennel-Fig Sauce makes a showy presentation for special dinner guests.

Chicky Kowloon

until duck and vegetables are tender. Remove duck to a platter, and keep warm. Reserve cooking liquid in slow cooker. Increase to high-heat setting.

3. Combine remaining ¼ cup port, cornstarch, and tomato paste in a small bowl; stir until well blended. Stir cornstarch mixture into cooking liquid in slow cooker. Cook, uncovered, 20 minutes or until thick, stirring frequently. Serve duck with sauce. Yield: 4 servings (serving size: 1 duck breast half and ¾ cup sauce).

Diabetic Exchanges: 1 Starch, 1 Veg, 1½ Fruit, 3 L Meat
Per serving: CAL 337 (14% from fat); PRO 25.6g; FAT 5.5g (sat 1.6g); CARB 48.6g; FIB 7.3g; CHOL 87mg; IRON 7.2mg; SOD 535mg; CALC 104mg

Chicky Kowloon

This Asian-inspired dish earned rave reviews from our test kitchens, receiving our highest rating. It gets its unusual title from the Kowloon peninsula in Hong Kong.

3   (6-ounce) skinless, bone-in chicken breast halves
6   (4-ounce) chicken thighs, skinned
¼   teaspoon salt
¼   teaspoon pepper
Cooking spray
1   (8¼-ounce) can sliced pineapple in heavy syrup, undrained
1   (8-ounce) can sliced water chestnuts, drained
1   cup fat-free, less-sodium chicken broth
¼   teaspoon ground ginger
1   garlic clove, minced
¼   cup low-sodium soy sauce
¼   cup cornstarch
1   tablespoon white vinegar
½   cup diagonally sliced green onions
6   cups hot cooked rice, cooked without salt or fat
6   tablespoons chow mein noodles

1. Sprinkle chicken breast halves and thighs with salt and pepper. Coat a large nonstick skillet with cooking spray, and place over medium-high heat until hot. Add half of chicken; cook 3 minutes on each side or until browned. Repeat procedure with remaining chicken. Place chicken in a 5-quart electric slow cooker.

2. Drain pineapple, reserving syrup. Quarter pineapple slices; arrange pineapple and water chestnuts over chicken. Combine reserved syrup, chicken broth, ginger, and garlic; stir well. Pour over chicken.

3. Cover with lid; cook on high-heat setting 1 hour. Reduce to low-heat setting, and cook 6 to 7 hours or until chicken is tender. Remove chicken from slow cooker with a slotted spoon; keep warm. Reserve cooking liquid in slow cooker. Increase to high-heat setting.

4. Combine soy sauce, cornstarch, and vinegar in a small bowl, stirring with a whisk until well blended. Stir cornstarch mixture and green onions into cooking liquid. Cook 10 minutes or until slightly thick, stirring frequently. Serve chicken and sauce over rice; top with chow mein noodles. Yield: 6 servings (serving size: 1 breast half or 2 thighs, 1 cup rice, ½ cup sauce, and 1 tablespoon chow mein noodles).

Diabetic Exchanges: 4 Starch, 3 V-L Meat or 3 L Meat
Per serving: CAL 449 (11% from fat); PRO 34.0g; FAT 5.1g (sat 1.2g); CARB 63.3g; FIB 2.7g; CHOL 96mg; IRON 9.8mg; SOD 728mg; CALC 32mg

Fruited Chicken and Wild Rice

6   (4-ounce) skinless, boneless chicken breast halves
¾   cup all-purpose flour
½   teaspoon salt
½   teaspoon ground red pepper
4   teaspoons vegetable oil, divided
1⅓ cups finely chopped dried apple rings
½   cup sweetened dried cranberries (such as Craisins)
1   medium onion, cut into thin wedges
3   garlic cloves, minced
2   cups chicken broth
¼   teaspoon ground allspice
3   cups hot cooked wild rice, cooked without salt or fat

1. Place each chicken breast half between 2 sheets of heavy-duty plastic wrap; flatten breast halves to ¼-inch thickness using a meat mallet or rolling pin. Discard plastic wrap.

2. Combine flour, salt, and red pepper in a pie plate or shallow dish; stir well. Dredge chicken in flour mixture, shaking off excess.

3. Heat 2 teaspoons oil in a large nonstick skillet over medium-high heat. Add half of chicken, and cook 4 minutes on each side or until browned. Remove chicken from skillet; set aside. Repeat procedure with remaining 2 teaspoons oil and chicken.

4. Place half of chicken in a 4-quart electric slow cooker; top with apple, cranberries, onion, and garlic. Add remaining half of chicken. Combine chicken broth and allspice; pour over chicken.

5. Cover with lid; cook on high-heat setting 1 hour. Reduce to low-heat setting, and cook 7 hours. Serve chicken and fruit sauce over wild rice. Yield: 6 servings (serving size: 1 chicken breast half, ⅔ cup fruit sauce, and ½ cup rice).

Diabetic Exchanges: 2½ Starch, 1 Fruit, 3 V-L Meat
Per serving: CAL 388 (13% from fat); PRO 32.3g; FAT 5.8g (sat 0.9g); CARB 51.8g; FIB 4.5g; CHOL 66mg; IRON 2.4mg; SOD 621mg; CALC 28mg

Rioja Chicken

3   tablespoons all-purpose flour
¼   teaspoon salt
¼   teaspoon pepper
8   chicken thighs (about 2½ pounds), skinned
5   garlic cloves, thinly sliced
½   cup pitted prunes
¼   cup pimiento-stuffed olives
2   tablespoons minced fresh or 2 teaspoons dried thyme
1   tablespoon grated lemon rind
1   bay leaf
1   cup orange juice
1   cup Rioja or other dry red wine
2   tablespoons honey
2   cups hot cooked long-grain rice, cooked without salt or fat
½   cup chopped fresh parsley

1. Combine first 3 ingredients in a shallow dish. Dredge chicken in flour mixture. Place garlic in a 3½- to 4½-quart electric slow cooker. Arrange chicken over garlic; add prunes and next 4 ingredients.

2. Combine orange juice, wine, and honey; pour over chicken. Cover with lid; cook on high-heat setting 1 hour. Reduce to low-heat setting, and cook 7 hours. Discard bay leaf. Serve chicken and sauce over rice; sprinkle with parsley. Yield: 4 servings (serving size: 2 thighs, 1 cup sauce, ½ cup rice, and 2 tablespoons parsley).

Diabetic Exchanges: 2½ Starch, 1½ Fruit, 3½ L Meat
Per serving: CAL 450 (19% from fat); PRO 33.2g; FAT 9.4g (sat 2.0g); CARB 58.7g; FIB 2.8g; CHOL 120mg; IRON 4.7mg; SOD 868mg; CALC 92mg

Sage and Prosciutto Cornish Hens ☺

Take care when removing hens from the slow cooker because they will be very tender.

2   (1½-pound) Cornish hens
1½ ounces very thinly sliced prosciutto
14   fresh sage leaves
1   small onion, quartered
½   cup fresh parsley sprigs
1   tangerine
½   teaspoon kosher salt
4   garlic cloves, crushed

1. Remove and discard giblets and necks from hens. Rinse hens under cold water; pat dry.

Loosen skin on breasts and legs with small scissors or a sharp knife. Place a single layer of prosciutto under skin over breast and legs (do not overlap). Arrange 1 sage leaf beneath skin on each hen leg. Arrange 5 sage leaves beneath skin on each breast. Gently press skin to secure. Place 2 onion wedges and ¼ cup parsley sprigs into each body cavity.

2. Grate 1 teaspoon rind from tangerine. Cut tangerine in half, and squeeze juice into a bowl. Place 1 tangerine half into each body cavity. Tie legs together with kitchen twine. Place a small rack, trivet, or 3 canning jar rings in bottom of a 4½-quart electric slow cooker. Place hens, breast side up, on rack; pour tangerine juice over hens.

3. Combine tangerine rind, salt, and garlic, stirring well to make a paste. Rub paste over hens. Cover with lid; cook on high-heat setting 1 hour. Reduce to low-heat setting, and cook 4 to 5 hours or until done. Split hens in half lengthwise; discard onion, parsley, and tangerine from body cavity. Discard skin. Yield: 4 servings (serving size: 1 hen half).

Diabetic Exchanges: ½ Veg, 5 V-L Meat, ½ L Meat
Per serving: CAL 226 (23% from fat); PRO 38.1g; FAT 5.7g (sat 1.7g); CARB 3.8g; FIB 0.5g; CHOL 120mg; IRON 2.6mg; SOD 388mg; CALC 66mg

Chicken Lasagna Florentine ⊘

2 (10¾-ounce) cans condensed reduced-fat, reduced-sodium cream of chicken soup, undiluted
1 (10-ounce) package frozen chopped spinach, thawed, drained, and squeezed dry
1 (9-ounce) package frozen diced cooked chicken (such as Tyson)
1 (8-ounce) carton reduced-fat sour cream (such as Breakstone)
1 cup 1% low-fat milk
½ cup (2 ounces) grated fresh Parmesan cheese
⅓ cup chopped onion
½ teaspoon salt
¼ teaspoon pepper
⅛ teaspoon ground nutmeg
9 uncooked lasagna noodles
Cooking spray
1 cup (4 ounces) shredded part-skim mozzarella cheese

1. Combine first 10 ingredients in a large bowl; stir well.

2. Place 3 uncooked lasagna noodles in bottom of a 5-quart electric slow cooker coated with cooking spray, breaking noodles in half as necessary to fit slow cooker. Spread one-third of spinach mixture over noodles; sprinkle with ⅓ cup mozzarella cheese. Layer 3 more noodles, half of remaining spinach mixture, and ⅓ cup mozzarella cheese. Top with remaining noodles and spinach mixture; sprinkle with remaining ⅓ cup mozzarella cheese.

3. Cover with lid; cook on high-heat setting 1 hour. Reduce to low-heat setting, and cook 5 hours or until pasta is done. Yield: 8 servings (serving size: about 1 cup).

Diabetic Exchanges: 2 Starch, 2 V-L Meat, 1 M-F Meat, 1 Fat
Per serving: CAL 339 (34% from fat); PRO 23.9g; FAT 12.5g (sat 6.7g); CARB 31.0g; FIB 2.0g; CHOL 62mg; IRON 2.1mg; SOD 729mg; CALC 334mg

Not only is Chicken Lasagna Florentine creamy and cheesy, it starts with uncooked noodles so cleanup is a breeze.

pork

Pork Chops and Gravy ⊘

Serve pork chops with mashed potatoes and gravy. Try Ore-Ida frozen mashed potatoes to save time.

6   (6-ounce) bone-in center-cut loin pork chops (about ½ inch thick)
1   tablespoon vegetable oil, divided
1   (14½-ounce) can chicken broth
1½ teaspoons dry mustard
¼   teaspoon salt
¼   teaspoon garlic powder
⅔   cup all-purpose flour
Freshly ground pepper (optional)

1. Trim fat from chops. Heat 1½ teaspoons oil in a large nonstick skillet over medium-high heat. Add 3 chops; cook 2 minutes on each side or until browned. Place chops in a 4½-quart electric slow cooker. Repeat procedure with remaining oil and pork chops.

2. Combine broth, mustard, salt, and garlic powder; stir well. Pour broth mixture over pork chops in slow cooker. Cover with lid; cook on high-heat setting 1 hour. Reduce to low-heat setting; cook 4 hours or until pork chops are tender. Remove pork chops from slow cooker, reserving cooking liquid. Set chops aside, and keep warm. Increase to high-heat setting.

3. Place flour in a small bowl. Gradually add 1 cup cooking liquid to flour, stirring with a whisk until well blended. Stir flour mixture into cooking liquid in slow cooker. Cook, uncovered, 10 minutes or until thick, stirring occasionally. Spoon gravy over chops; sprinkle with pepper, if desired. Yield: 6 servings (serving size: 1 chop and about ⅓ cup gravy).

Diabetic Exchanges: ½ Starch, 3½ L Meat, ½ Fat
Per serving: CAL 227 (42% from fat); PRO 27.1g; FAT 10.4g (sat 3.1g); CARB 4.6g; FIB 0.2g; CHOL 73mg; IRON 1.2mg; SOD 453mg; CALC 23mg

Firecracker Pork with Fruity Lime Salsa

1   (5-pound) boneless Boston Butt pork roast
1   tablespoon paprika
1   teaspoon dried thyme
½   teaspoon salt
½   teaspoon pepper
6   garlic cloves, minced
¾   cup water
1   (7-ounce) can chipotle chiles in adobo sauce, undrained
1   small onion, cut into 1-inch chunks
16 (8-inch) flour tortillas
Fruity Lime Salsa
Fresh cilantro leaves (optional)

1. Trim fat from roast; cut roast in half crosswise. Combine paprika and next 4 ingredients; stir well. Rub spice mixture over surface of roast halves; place roast halves in a 6-quart electric slow cooker. Combine water, chipotle chiles, and onion in a food processor or blender; process until smooth. Pour chile puree over pork. Cover with lid; cook on high-heat setting 1 hour. Reduce to low heat-setting, and cook 9 hours or until pork is very tender.

2. Remove pork from slow cooker; let stand 10 minutes. Shred pork with 2 forks; set aside.

3. Pour cooking liquid into a bowl; let stand 5 minutes. Skim fat from surface of liquid. Return cooking liquid and shredded pork to slow cooker; stir well. Cover with lid, and cook on high-heat setting 15 minutes or until warm. Serve pork in flour tortillas with Fruity Lime Salsa. Garnish with fresh cilantro leaves, if desired. Yield: 16 servings (serving size: 1 tortilla, ½ cup pork mixture, and about 3½ tablespoons salsa).

Diabetic Exchanges: 1½ Starch, 2 Veg, 3 M-F Meat
Per serving: CAL 374 (33% from fat); PRO 29.7g; FAT 13.6g (sat 4.2g); CARB 31.8g; FIB 1.5g; CHOL 87mg; IRON 3.0mg; SOD 469mg; CALC 140mg

Fruity Lime Salsa:

1   (8-ounce) can crushed pineapple, drained
2   cups diced peeled papaya
1   cup diced peeled kiwifruit
⅓   cup finely chopped red onion
½   cup chopped fresh cilantro
3   tablespoons fresh lime juice

1. Combine all ingredients in a bowl; stir well. Cover and chill 2 to 24 hours. Yield: 3½ cups (serving size: about 3½ tablespoons).

Firecracker Pork with
Fruity Lime Salsa

3. Spread stuffing mixture over roast. Reroll roast; secure at 1-inch intervals with heavy string. Sprinkle salt over roast; coat with cooking spray.

4. Place a large nonstick skillet over medium-high heat until hot. Add roast, browning on all sides. Place roast in a 3½-quart electric slow cooker; top with onion slices and apple rings. Cover with lid; cook on high-heat setting 1 hour. Reduce to low-heat setting, and cook 3 hours or until roast is tender. Remove roast, onion slices, and apple rings to a serving platter; set aside, and keep warm.

5. Place flour in a small saucepan. Gradually add remaining 1 tablespoon bourbon, remaining 1 tablespoon maple syrup, and apple juice, stirring until well blended. Place over medium heat, and cook until thick and bubbly, stirring frequently. Cut roast into 8 slices. Serve roast with onion slices, apple rings, and sauce. Yield: 8 servings (serving size: 1 slice pork, 1 apple ring, 1 onion slice, and about 2 tablespoons sauce).

Diabetic Exchanges: 2 Starch, 3 L Meat
Per serving: CAL 319 (27% from fat); PRO 27.8g; FAT 9.4g (sat 2.5g); CARB 27.2g; FIB 2.3g; CHOL 62mg; IRON 2.1mg; SOD 454mg; CALC 52mg

Cabbage Rolls ⊘

12 large green cabbage leaves
3 cups chopped onion
½ cup uncooked instant rice
½ pound lean ground pork
½ pound 97% fat-free pork breakfast sausage (such as Jimmy Dean)
¼ teaspoon pepper
1 (10-ounce) can shredded sauerkraut, drained
½ teaspoon caraway seeds
2 cups tomato juice
2 tablespoons brown sugar
3 tablespoons tomato paste

1. Cook cabbage leaves in boiling water 6 minutes or just until tender. Drain and set aside. Reserve remaining cabbage for another use.

2. Place a nonstick skillet over medium heat until hot. Add onion; sauté 5 minutes or until tender. Remove from heat; stir in rice. Let cool 15 minutes.

Serve asparagus with lemon zest alongside Pecan-Corn Bread Stuffed Pork for a special Sunday meal.

Pecan-Corn Bread Stuffed Pork ⊘

1 (2-pound) rolled lean boneless pork loin roast
1 cup seasoned corn bread stuffing mix
2½ tablespoons bourbon, divided
2 tablespoons pure maple syrup, divided
½ cup finely chopped peeled Granny Smith apple
½ cup finely chopped Vidalia onion or other sweet onion
¼ cup chopped pecans
1½ tablespoons water
¼ teaspoon rubbed sage
⅛ teaspoon dried thyme
⅛ teaspoon pepper
¼ teaspoon salt
Cooking spray
8 (¼-inch-thick) slices Vidalia onion or other sweet onion
8 (¼-inch-thick) rings Granny Smith apple
3 tablespoons all-purpose flour
¾ cup apple juice

1. Unroll roast; trim fat from roast.

2. Combine stuffing mix, 1½ tablespoons bourbon, 1 tablespoon maple syrup, ½ cup apple, and next 6 ingredients in a large bowl; toss well.

3. Combine rice mixture, pork, sausage, and pepper; stir well. Spoon about ¼ cup mixture into center of each cabbage leaf. Fold left and right sides of leaf over filling, and roll up, beginning with 1 short end.

4. Combine sauerkraut and caraway seeds; stir well. Spoon half of sauerkraut mixture into a 3½- to 4-quart electric slow cooker. Top with half of cabbage rolls, seam sides down. Repeat layers with remaining sauerkraut mixture and cabbage rolls. Combine tomato juice, brown sugar, and tomato paste; stir well with a whisk. Pour tomato juice mixture over cabbage rolls. Cover with lid; cook on high-heat setting 1 hour. Reduce to low-heat setting, and cook 4½ hours or until done (pork will be pink in color even when it is done). Yield: 6 servings (serving size: 2 cabbage rolls and about ½ cup sauerkraut mixture).

Diabetic Exchanges: 1 Starch, 2 Veg, 1½ M-F Meat
Per serving: CAL 263 (34% from fat); PRO 15.7g; FAT 9.4g (sat 3.3g); CARB 25.9g; FIB 4.3g; CHOL 46mg; IRON 2.1mg; SOD 723mg; CALC 57mg

Golden Fruited Ham Steak

A hint of vinegar and Dijon mustard balances the sweet spices and fruit in this family-friendly dish.

1 (2-pound) slice reduced-sodium, fully cooked ham (about ¾ inch thick)
1 (12-ounce) jar apricot preserves
¼ cup firmly packed light brown sugar
2 tablespoons all-purpose flour
1 tablespoon white wine vinegar
1 tablespoon Dijon mustard
½ teaspoon ground ginger
⅛ teaspoon ground cloves
1 (15-ounce) can apricot halves in juice, drained and coarsely chopped
½ cup golden raisins
2 tablespoons cornstarch
2 tablespoons water

1. Trim fat from ham. Place ham in a 4-quart electric slow cooker.

2. Combine preserves and next 6 ingredients; stir well. Stir in chopped apricots and raisins; pour mixture over ham. Cover with lid; cook on high-heat setting 2 hours or until ham is thoroughly heated.

3. Remove ham from slow cooker; keep warm. Pour cooking liquid into a small saucepan. Combine cornstarch and water in a small bowl; stir well. Add cornstarch mixture to cooking liquid. Bring to a boil, and cook 1 minute or until thick, stirring constantly. Serve sauce with ham. Yield: 6 servings (serving size: 3 ounces ham and about ½ cup sauce).

Diabetic Exchanges: 4 Starch, ½ Fruit, 3 L Meat
Per serving: CAL 415 (14% from fat); PRO 24.9g; FAT 6.6g (sat 2.1g); CARB 65.7g; FIB 1.0g; CHOL 60mg; IRON 2.3mg; SOD 1,199mg; CALC 28mg

Green Chile Soup

1½ pounds lean boneless pork loin roast
3 (4.5-ounce) cans chopped green chiles, undrained
1 (15-ounce) can pinto beans, undrained
1 (14½-ounce) can stewed tomatoes, undrained and chopped
2½ cups chopped onion
2 cups water
1 teaspoon salt
¼ teaspoon ground cumin
¼ teaspoon dried oregano
1 garlic clove, minced
⅔ cup 30%-less-fat sour cream (such as Breakstone)
⅔ cup (2⅔ ounces) shredded Cheddar cheese
⅔ cup diced peeled avocado
⅔ cup sliced green onions

1. Trim fat from pork; cut pork into 1-inch cubes. Combine pork, chiles, beans, tomatoes, onion, water, salt, cumin, oregano, and garlic in a 3½- to 4-quart electric slow cooker. Cover with lid; cook on high-heat setting 1 hour. Reduce to low-heat setting, and cook 6 hours or until pork is tender. Ladle soup into bowls; top with sour cream, cheese, avocado, and green onions. Yield: 10 servings (serving size: 1 cup soup, about 1 tablespoon sour cream, about 1 tablespoon cheese, about 1 tablespoon avocado, and about 1 tablespoon green onions).

Diabetic Exchanges: ½ Starch, 2 Veg, 2½ L Meat, 1 Fat
Per serving: CAL 243 (34% from fat); PRO 21.2g; FAT 9.3g (sat 4.2g); CARB 18.9g; FIB 3.8g; CHOL 59mg; IRON 2.6mg; SOD 562mg; CALC 133mg

SLOW SECRETS

Follow these secrets for slow cooker success.

1 Read the instruction booklet that comes with your appliance.

2 Slow cookers come in sizes ranging from 16 ounces to 6 quarts. The 16-ounce and 1-quart slow cookers have no low-heat setting or high-heat setting, only off and on.

3 For the best results, choose the right size slow cooker for the recipe, and always fill the slow cooker at least half full. Recipes with a lot of liquid, such as a soup, will usually work fine in a variety of different size slow cookers. However, recipes with less liquid may burn if cooked in a larger slow cooker for the full amount of time. If you are using a larger slow cooker than recommended, watch the cook time closely.

4 Coat the inside of the crockery insert with cooking spray to make cleanup easier and quicker.

5 Always cook with the lid on, and don't lift the lid until it's time to stir or until the end of the recommended cook time.

6 One hour on high-heat setting equals 2 to 2½ hours on low-heat setting. There's no need to preheat a slow cooker.

7 Layer the ingredients in the slow cooker as directed to ensure that they get tender. Ingredients on the bottom cook faster.

Italian Pot Roast with Artichokes
and Potatoes

Italian Pot Roast with Artichokes and Potatoes

The cut of pork used in this recipe looks much like a rack of chops. To ensure even cooking, cut the roast in half through the center two bones.

1   (3-pound) bone-in center-cut pork loin roast
4   teaspoons dried Italian seasoning
1   teaspoon salt, divided
½   teaspoon pepper
2   teaspoons olive oil
½   cup chopped onion
3   garlic cloves, minced
¼   cup chicken broth
9   small red potatoes (about 1 pound), halved
12 kalamata olives
1   tablespoon capers
1   teaspoon dried oregano
2   (14-ounce) cans whole artichoke hearts (5 to 7 count), drained
Oregano sprigs (optional)

1. Trim fat from roast; cut roast in half. Combine Italian seasoning, ½ teaspoon salt, and pepper; rub over surface of roast halves. Heat oil in a large nonstick skillet over medium-high heat. Add roast halves; cook 8 minutes, browning on all sides. Remove roast halves from skillet, and place in a 6-quart electric slow cooker. Add onion and garlic to skillet. Place over medium heat, and sauté 5 minutes. Add broth, scraping skillet to loosen browned bits. Pour mixture over roast in slow cooker.

2. Arrange potatoes and olives around roast; sprinkle with remaining ½ teaspoon salt, capers, and oregano. Cover with lid; cook on high-heat setting 1 hour. Reduce to low-heat setting, and cook 7 hours. Add artichoke hearts, and cook an additional 1 hour.

3. Place roast on a large platter. Arrange vegetables, olives, and capers around roast. Garnish with oregano sprigs, if desired. Yield: 6 servings (serving size: 3 ounces pork, 3 potato halves, about 2 artichoke hearts, and 2 olives).

Diabetic Exchanges: 1 Starch, 2 Veg, 3 L Meat, ½ Fat
Per serving: CAL 313 (33% from fat); PRO 27.5g; FAT 11.4g (sat 3.4g); CARB 23.8g; FIB 2.4g; CHOL 67mg; IRON 3.5mg; SOD 857mg; CALC 59mg

Pork 'n' Slaw Sandwiches

1   (3-pound) lean boneless pork loin roast
1   cup water
1   (18-ounce) bottle barbecue sauce
2   tablespoons brown sugar
1½   tablespoons hot sauce
½   teaspoon salt
½   teaspoon pepper
2½   cups prepackaged cabbage-and-carrot coleslaw
⅓   cup light coleslaw dressing (such as Marzetti)
15   (2-ounce) hamburger buns

1. Trim fat from roast. Place roast and water in a 4-quart electric slow cooker. Cover with lid; cook on high-heat setting 7 hours or until meat is tender. Drain pork, discarding cooking liquid. Return pork to slow cooker, and shred with 2 forks.

2. Add barbecue sauce and next 4 ingredients to pork in slow cooker; stir well. Reduce to low-heat setting; cover and cook 1 hour.

3. Combine coleslaw and dressing in a bowl; toss well. Serve barbecue on buns with coleslaw. Yield: 15 servings (serving size: 1 bun, ⅓ cup barbecue, and about 2 tablespoons coleslaw).

Diabetic Exchanges: 2½ Starch, 2½ L Meat, ½ Fat
Per serving: CAL 331 (26% from fat); PRO 22.2g; FAT 9.7g (sat 2.8g); CARB 38.1g; FIB 2.3g; CHOL 51mg; IRON 2.4mg; SOD 835mg; CALC 75mg

Tea-Braised Pork Tenderloin with Cherries

1   (1¾-pound) pork tenderloin
½   teaspoon salt
½   teaspoon pepper
1   teaspoon olive oil
1   medium onion, quartered
½   cup strongly brewed tea
¼   cup red currant jelly
¼   cup chili sauce
2   teaspoons brown sugar
1   teaspoon balsamic vinegar
⅛   teaspoon ground red pepper
1   cup pitted fresh bing cherries
1   teaspoon chopped fresh chives

1. Trim fat from tenderloin; rub surface of tenderloin with salt and pepper. Heat oil in a large nonstick skillet over medium-high heat. Add pork;

Grilled pineapple slices are a tasty side dish for our top-rated Caribbean-Style Pork.

cook 8 minutes, turning to brown all sides. Remove pork from skillet; place pork and onion in a 4-quart electric slow cooker. Add tea to skillet, scraping to loosen browned bits. Cook over high heat 1 minute. Pour tea mixture over pork in slow cooker. Cover with lid; cook on high-heat setting 1 hour. Reduce to low-heat setting, and cook 6 hours.

2. Remove pork from slow cooker; set aside, and keep warm. Pour cooking liquid into a small saucepan; bring to a boil. Reduce heat to medium-high, and cook 8 minutes or until mixture is reduced to ½ cup. Add red currant jelly and next 4 ingredients; cook 1 minute or until jelly melts, stirring frequently. Stir in cherries, and cook 1 minute or until warm. Pour mixture over pork; sprinkle with chives. Yield: 7 servings (serving size: 3 ounces pork and about 3 tablespoons sauce).

Diabetic Exchanges: 1 Starch, 3 L Meat
Per serving: CAL 210 (22% from fat); PRO 24.3g; FAT 5.0g (sat 1.6g); CARB 16.1g; FIB 0.7g; CHOL 67mg; IRON 1.4mg; SOD 495mg; CALC 12mg

Caribbean-Style Pork

2   pounds lean boneless center-cut pork loin roast
1   teaspoon olive oil
2   cups chopped red bell pepper
6   green onions, cut into 1-inch pieces
Cooking spray
2   tablespoons hoisin sauce
1   tablespoon low-sodium soy sauce
1   tablespoon fresh lime juice
2   tablespoons creamy peanut butter
1   teaspoon cumin seed, crushed
½   teaspoon salt
½   teaspoon crushed red pepper
2   garlic cloves, minced
4½ cups hot cooked basmati rice, cooked without salt or fat
2   tablespoons diagonally sliced green onions

1. Trim fat from roast; cut roast into 1-inch pieces. Heat oil in a large nonstick skillet over medium heat. Add pork; sauté 5 minutes or until browned.

2. Place pork, bell pepper, and green onions in a 4-quart electric slow cooker coated with cooking spray; stir well.

3. Combine hoisin sauce and next 7 ingredients in a small bowl; stir until well blended. Pour mixture over pork; stir well.

4. Cover with lid; cook on high-heat setting 1 hour. Reduce to low-heat setting, and cook 5 to 6 hours. Serve over rice; sprinkle with green onions. Yield: 6 servings (serving size: ¾ cup rice, ⅔ cup pork mixture, and 1 teaspoon green onions).

Diabetic Exchanges: 2½ Starch, 1 Veg, 4 L Meat
Per serving: CAL 402 (21% from fat); PRO 35.8g; FAT 9.4g (sat 2.6g); CARB 41.4g; FIB 2.3g; CHOL 85mg; IRON 3.6mg; SOD 470mg; CALC 32mg

Cranberry Pork Roast

Serve with couscous and steamed broccoli.

1   (3-pound) lean boneless pork loin roast
Cooking spray
1   (16-ounce) can whole-berry cranberry sauce
1   tablespoon brown sugar
1   teaspoon yellow mustard
2   tablespoons cornstarch
2   tablespoons water

1. Trim fat from roast; cut roast in half crosswise. Coat roast halves with cooking spray. Place a large nonstick skillet over medium-high heat until hot. Add roast halves, browning on all sides. Place roast halves in a 4-quart electric slow cooker coated with cooking spray.

2. Combine cranberry sauce, brown sugar, and mustard; pour over roast. Cover with lid; cook on high-heat setting 1 hour. Reduce to low-heat setting, and cook 6 hours. Remove roast from slow cooker, reserving cranberry mixture in cooker. Set roast aside; keep warm.

3. Combine cornstarch and water in a 1-quart glass measure or bowl; stir with a whisk until well blended. Gradually stir reserved cranberry mixture into cornstarch mixture. Microwave at HIGH 2 minutes or until thick, stirring after 1 minute. Serve sauce with roast. Yield: 12 servings (serving size: 3 ounces roast and about ¼ cup sauce).

Diabetic Exchanges: 1 Fruit, 3½ L Meat
Per serving: CAL 241 (31% from fat); PRO 24.4g; FAT 8.2g (sat 3.0g); CARB 16.4g; FIB 0.6g; CHOL 69mg; IRON 1.0mg; SOD 63mg; CALC 17mg

Pinto Beans with Ham

Boiling and letting the beans stand is necessary to make sure they get tender in the slow cooker. Serve with plenty of bread for soaking up the juices.

1 pound dried pinto beans
5½ cups water
1½ cups chopped onion
⅔ cup chopped lean cooked ham (about ¼ pound)
1 tablespoon chili powder
1 teaspoon pepper
¼ teaspoon dried oregano
¼ teaspoon ground cumin
1 garlic clove, minced
1½ teaspoons salt

1. Sort and wash beans; place beans in a large Dutch oven. Cover with water to 2 inches above beans. Bring to a boil, and cook 1 minute. Remove from heat; cover and let stand 1 hour. Drain beans well.

2. Place beans in a 5-quart electric slow cooker. Add 5½ cups water and next 7 ingredients; stir well. Cover with lid; cook on low-heat setting 10 hours or until beans are tender. Stir in salt. Yield: 8 servings (serving size: 1 cup).

Diabetic Exchanges: 2 Starch, 1 Veg, 2 V-L Meat
Per serving: CAL 216 (7% from fat); PRO 14.2g; FAT 1.6g (sat 0.4g); CARB 37.6g; FIB 12.4g; CHOL 7mg; IRON 3.9mg; SOD 657mg; CALC 79mg

Barbecue Pork Chops ⊘

8 (6-ounce) bone-in center-cut loin pork chops
¼ teaspoon pepper
⅛ teaspoon salt
Cooking spray
½ cup thick-and-spicy honey barbecue sauce (such as Kraft)
1 (14.5-ounce) can stewed tomatoes, undrained
1 (10-ounce) package frozen vegetable seasoning blend (such as McKenzie's)
¼ teaspoon salt

1. Trim fat from chops; sprinkle chops with pepper and ⅛ teaspoon salt. Coat chops with

Pinto Beans with Ham, coleslaw, and drop biscuits satisfy the craving for a country-style meal.

cooking spray. Place a large nonstick skillet over medium-high heat until hot. Add 4 chops; cook 3 minutes on each side or until browned. Remove chops from skillet; set aside. Repeat procedure with remaining 4 chops. Coat a 3½- to 4-quart electric slow cooker with cooking spray. Place chops in slow cooker.

2. Combine barbecue sauce, tomatoes, vegetable seasoning blend, and ¼ teaspoon salt; stir well. Pour mixture over chops. Cover with lid; cook on high-heat setting 1 hour. Reduce to low-heat setting, and cook 4 hours or until tender. Serve chops with sauce. Yield: 8 servings (serving size: 1 chop and ½ cup sauce).

Diabetic Exchanges: ½ Starch, 1 Veg, 3½ L Meat
Per serving: CAL 231 (29% from fat); PRO 26.1g; FAT 7.2g (sat 2.7g); CARB 12.7g; FIB 0.8g; CHOL 73mg; IRON 1.1mg; SOD 496mg; CALC 28mg

Rosemary-Fennel Pork with Potatoes

The fragrant, needle-shaped leaves of rosemary lend a lemon-pine flavor to this dish.

2 tablespoons fresh rosemary leaves
1 tablespoon fennel seeds
1 tablespoon dry white wine
2 teaspoons salt
1 teaspoon cracked black pepper
10 large garlic cloves, peeled
1 (3-pound) lean boneless pork loin roast
1 teaspoon olive oil
Cooking spray
27 small red potatoes (about 3¼ pounds), unpeeled
⅓ cup water

1. Combine first 6 ingredients in a food processor; process 1 minute or until a thick paste forms, scraping sides of processor bowl once. Set garlic-herb paste aside.

2. Trim fat from pork; cut pork roast in half crosswise. Using a sharp knife, cut slits, about 1 inch wide and 1 inch deep, at 2-inch intervals over entire surface of roast halves. Fill in slits with garlic-herb paste.

3. Heat oil in a nonstick skillet over medium-high heat. Add roast; cook 5 minutes, browning well.

4. Place roast halves in a 6-quart electric slow cooker coated with cooking spray; place potatoes around roast. Add ⅓ cup water to slow cooker. Cover with lid; cook on high-heat setting 1 hour. Reduce to low-heat setting, and cook 6 to 7 hours or until roast is tender.

5. Remove roast and potatoes to a serving platter; keep warm. Pour cooking liquid into a bowl; let stand 5 minutes. Skim fat from surface of liquid. Slice pork; serve pork and potatoes with cooking liquid. Yield: 9 servings (serving size: 3 ounces pork, 3 potatoes, and about 2 tablespoons cooking liquid).

Diabetic Exchanges: 2½ Starch, 3 L Meat
Per serving: CAL 303 (17% from fat); PRO 27.3g; FAT 5.6g (sat 1.8g); CARB 35.2g; FIB 3.6g; CHOL 71mg; IRON 3.0mg; SOD 587mg; CALC 44mg

Spiced Pork

The combination of cinnamon, cloves, tomato, onion, and jalapeños gives these shredded pork sandwiches plenty of flavor.

1 (2-pound) lean boneless pork loin roast
2 (14½-ounce) cans diced tomatoes, drained
2 cups chopped onion
1 tablespoon chopped pickled jalapeño peppers
2 tablespoons cider vinegar
2 tablespoons tomato paste
1 teaspoon beef bouillon granules
¼ teaspoon salt
¼ teaspoon ground cinnamon
⅛ teaspoon ground cloves
10 (2-ounce) hamburger buns, toasted

1. Trim fat from roast; cut into 2-inch pieces. Place pork and next 9 ingredients in a 4-quart electric slow cooker; stir well. Cover with lid; cook on high-heat setting 1 hour. Reduce to low-heat setting, and cook 8 hours or until roast is tender.

2. Shred pork with 2 forks. Serve with a slotted spoon on toasted buns. Yield: 10 servings (serving size: ½ cup pork and 1 bun).

Diabetic Exchanges: 2 Starch, 1 Veg, 2½ L Meat
Per serving: CAL 310 (21% from fat); PRO 25.5g; FAT 7.3g (sat 2.3g); CARB 34.9g; FIB 2.7g; CHOL 50mg; IRON 2.4mg; SOD 629mg; CALC 92mg

Sunday Ham with Lemon and Ginger ⟳

Look for lemon curd next to the jam and jelly in larger supermarkets.

1   (3-pound) boneless, fully cooked ham
22 whole cloves
1   teaspoon pepper
½   cup ginger ale
½   cup prepared lemon curd
2   tablespoons minced crystallized ginger
Lemon wedges (optional)
Flat-leaf parsley sprigs (optional)

1. Score outside of ham in a diamond pattern; stud with cloves. Sprinkle with pepper. Place ham in a 3½-quart electric slow cooker; pour ginger ale around ham. Combine lemon curd and ginger; stir well. Brush half of lemon curd mixture over ham; cover and chill remaining lemon curd mixture. Cover with lid; cook on high-heat setting 1 hour. Reduce to low-heat setting, and cook 4 hours.

2. Brush remaining lemon curd mixture over ham. Cover with lid; cook on high-heat setting an additional 30 minutes. Remove ham to a serving platter. Let stand 15 minutes before slicing. Serve with cooking liquid. Garnish with lemon wedges and parsley sprigs, if desired. Yield: 15 servings (serving size: 3 ounces ham and about 1 tablespoon ginger ale mixture).

Diabetic Exchanges: ½ Starch, 3 L Meat
Per serving: CAL 182 (36% from fat); PRO 19.1g; FAT 7.2g (sat 2.5g); CARB 9.4g; FIB 1.1g; CHOL 58mg; IRON 1.3mg; SOD 1,213mg; CALC 8mg

Picante Pork Chops

8   (6-ounce) bone-in center-cut loin pork chops
Cooking spray
1   (16-ounce) jar thick and chunky picante sauce
8   cups hot cooked saffron yellow rice mix, cooked without salt or fat

1. Trim fat from chops; coat chops with cooking spray. Place a large nonstick skillet over medium-high heat until hot. Add 4 chops; cook 3 minutes

Infused with flavor from hours of slow cooking, Sunday Ham with Lemon and Ginger takes on the texture of a fresh ham.

Chinese Pork Tenderloin with
Garlic-Sauced Noodles

on each side or until browned. Remove chops from skillet; set aside. Repeat procedure with remaining 4 chops.

2. Pour one-fourth of picante sauce into a 4-quart electric slow cooker coated with cooking spray; arrange chops over sauce. Pour remaining picante sauce over chops. Cover with lid; cook on high-heat setting 1 hour. Reduce to low-heat setting, and cook 5 to 7 hours. Remove chops from slow cooker, reserving 1 cup picante sauce mixture from cooker. Discard remaining picante sauce mixture. Serve chops over rice; top each serving with reserved picante sauce mixture. Yield: 8 servings (serving size: 1 chop, 1 cup rice, and 2 tablespoons picante sauce mixture).

Diabetic Exchanges: 2½ Starch, 1 Veg, 3 L Meat
Per serving: CAL 383 (17% from fat); PRO 29.7g; FAT 7.2g (sat 2.7g); CARB 46.8g; FIB 1.0g; CHOL 73mg; IRON 2.8mg; SOD 1,288mg; CALC 60mg

Chinese Pork Tenderloin with Garlic-Sauced Noodles ⊘

2 (1-pound) pork tenderloins
1 tablespoon hoisin sauce
1 tablespoon tomato sauce
1 tablespoon low-sodium soy sauce
1 teaspoon sugar
2 teaspoons minced fresh garlic
1 teaspoon grated peeled fresh ginger
¼ cup low-sodium soy sauce
¼ cup seasoned rice vinegar
1 teaspoon dark sesame oil
8 cups hot cooked Chinese egg noodles or vermicelli (about 16 ounces uncooked), cooked without salt or fat
1 cup shredded carrot
¾ cup diagonally sliced green onions
¼ cup fresh cilantro leaves
⅓ cup chopped dry-roasted peanuts
⅓ cup chopped fresh cilantro

1. Trim fat from tenderloins; place tenderloins in a 4½-quart electric slow cooker. Combine hoisin sauce and next 5 ingredients; stir well, and drizzle over tenderloins in slow cooker. Cover with lid; cook on high-heat setting 1 hour. Reduce to low-heat setting, and cook 5 hours. Remove pork from slow cooker, reserving cooking liquid. Let pork stand 10 minutes.

2. Pour cooking liquid into a bowl; let stand 15 minutes. Skim fat from surface of liquid. Wipe out inside of crockery insert with paper towels. Shred pork with 2 forks. Combine shredded pork and ¼ cup cooking liquid in a bowl; toss well. Cover and set aside. Return remaining cooking liquid to slow cooker; stir in ¼ cup soy sauce, ¼ cup vinegar, and sesame oil. Cover with lid; cook on high-heat setting 10 minutes. Add hot noodles, carrot, green onions, and cilantro leaves to slow cooker; toss to coat. Cover and let stand 3 minutes.

3. Serve pork over noodle mixture; sprinkle with peanuts and chopped cilantro. Yield: 8 servings (serving size: 1¼ cups noodle mixture, ⅔ cup pork, 2 teaspoons peanuts, and 2 teaspoons cilantro).

Diabetic Exchanges: 3 Starch, 1 Veg, 3 L Meat, ½ Fat
Per serving: CAL 398 (20% from fat); PRO 32.3g; FAT 9.3g (sat 2.3g); CARB 48.8g; FIB 8.9g; CHOL 72mg; IRON 3.9mg; SOD 853mg; CALC 38mg

Braised Pork Loin with Port and Prunes

1 (3¼-pound) lean boneless pork loin roast
1½ teaspoons freshly ground pepper
1 teaspoon salt
1 teaspoon dry mustard
1 teaspoon dried sage (not rubbed sage)
½ teaspoon dried thyme
1 tablespoon olive oil
2 cups sliced onion
1 cup finely chopped leek
1 cup finely chopped carrot
½ cup port or other sweet red wine
⅓ cup fat-free, less-sodium chicken broth
⅓ cup water
1 cup pitted prunes (about 20 prunes)
2 bay leaves
2 tablespoons cornstarch
2 tablespoons water

1. Trim fat from roast; cut roast in half crosswise. Combine pepper and next 4 ingredients; rub seasoning mixture over surface of roast halves.

2. Heat oil in a large Dutch oven over medium-high heat. Add pork, browning on all sides. Place pork in a 4½-quart electric slow cooker. Add onion, leek, and carrot to Dutch oven; sauté 5 minutes or until vegetables are golden. Stir in wine, broth, and ⅓ cup water, scraping pan to loosen browned bits. Pour wine mixture over pork in slow cooker; add prunes and bay leaves. Cover with lid; cook on high-heat setting 1 hour. Reduce to low-heat setting, and cook 5 to 6 hours or until pork is tender.

3. Remove pork from slow cooker; reserve cooking liquid in cooker. Set pork aside; keep warm. Increase to high-heat setting. Combine cornstarch and 2 tablespoons water; stir well, and add to cooking liquid. Cook, uncovered, 15 minutes or until mixture is thick, stirring frequently. Discard bay leaves. Slice pork, and serve with sauce. Yield: 10 servings (serving size: 3 ounces pork and ½ cup sauce).

Diabetic Exchanges: 1 Veg, 1 Fruit, 3½ L Meat
Per serving: CAL 251 (31% from fat); PRO 25.8g; FAT 8.7g (sat 2.7g); CARB 17.1g; FIB 2.3g; CHOL 73mg; IRON 1.9mg; SOD 310mg; CALC 41mg

Smoked Sausage Cassoulet is the perfect cold-weather party dish when served with wine, a green salad, and lots of crusty bread.

Smoked Sausage Cassoulet ⊙

For a thicker consistency, let the cassoulet stand 30 minutes before serving.

1   pound lean boneless pork loin roast
2   bacon slices
2   cups chopped onion
1   teaspoon dried thyme
½   teaspoon dried rosemary
3   garlic cloves, minced
1   teaspoon salt
½   teaspoon pepper
2   (14.5-ounce) cans diced tomatoes, drained
2   (15-ounce) cans Great Northern beans, rinsed and drained
½   pound low-fat smoked sausage, cut into ½-inch cubes
8   teaspoons finely shredded fresh Parmesan cheese
8   teaspoons chopped fresh flat-leaf parsley

1. Trim fat from pork; cut pork into 1-inch cubes. Cook bacon in a large skillet over medium-high heat until crisp. Remove bacon from skillet; crumble and set aside. Add onion, thyme, rosemary, and garlic to bacon drippings in skillet; sauté 3 minutes or until tender. Stir in crumbled bacon, salt, pepper, and tomatoes; bring to a boil. Remove from heat; set aside.

2. Mash half of beans with a potato masher until chunky. Combine mashed beans, remaining half of beans, pork loin, and sausage; stir well. Place half of bean mixture in a 3½-quart electric slow cooker; top with half of tomato mixture. Repeat layers. Cover with lid; cook on high-heat setting 1 hour. Reduce to low-heat setting, and cook 4 hours. Sprinkle Parmesan cheese and parsley over each serving. Yield: 8 servings (serving size: 1 cup cassoulet, 1 teaspoon cheese, and 1 teaspoon parsley).

Diabetic Exchanges: 1 Starch, 1 Veg, 2½ L Meat
Per serving: CAL 230 (33% from fat); PRO 20.2g; FAT 8.5g (sat 3.2g); CARB 17.7g; FIB 3.7g; CHOL 52mg; IRON 2.0mg; SOD 731mg; CALC 91mg

Asian Pork Loin

1   (2-pound) lean boneless center-cut pork loin roast
¾   cup orange juice
¼   cup low-salt soy sauce
1   tablespoon grated peeled fresh ginger

1   tablespoon minced fresh garlic
2   teaspoons crushed red pepper
1   teaspoon five spice powder
¼   teaspoon salt
2   tablespoons cornstarch
2   tablespoons water

1. Trim fat from roast. Combine orange juice and next 6 ingredients in a large zip-top plastic bag. Add pork; seal bag, and marinate in refrigerator 8 to 24 hours.

2. Place pork and marinade in a 4½-quart electric slow cooker. Cover with lid; cook on high-heat setting 1 hour. Reduce to low-heat setting, and cook 7 hours.

3. Remove pork from cooker; let stand 10 minutes before slicing. Pour cooking liquid into a 4-cup glass measure or bowl; let stand 5 minutes. Skim fat from surface of liquid. Combine cornstarch and water in a small bowl; stir until well blended. Add cornstarch mixture to cooking liquid; stir well. Microwave at HIGH 3 minutes or until slightly thick, stirring after 1½ minutes.

4. Slice pork; serve with sauce. Yield: 7 servings (serving size: 3 ounces pork and 3 tablespoons sauce).

Diabetic Exchanges: ½ Starch, 3½ L Meat
Per serving: CAL 217 (37% from fat); PRO 26.6g; FAT 8.6g (sat 3.1g); CARB 6.5g; FIB 0.3g; CHOL 74mg; IRON 1.3mg; SOD 491mg; CALC 33mg

Pork Chops with Sauerkraut and Caraway ⊘

2   (10-ounce) cans shredded sauerkraut
Cooking spray
1   (14.5-ounce) can diced tomatoes, drained
½   teaspoon caraway seeds
¼   teaspoon pepper
2   bay leaves
6   (6-ounce) bone-in center-cut loin pork
     chops
1   teaspoon olive oil, divided
1   (22-ounce) bag frozen mashed potatoes
     (such as Ore-Ida)
2⅓ cups fat-free milk

1. Drain sauerkraut, reserving ¼ cup juice. Place drained sauerkraut in a 3½-quart electric slow

cooker coated with cooking spray. Add tomatoes, caraway seeds, pepper, and bay leaves; stir well.

2. Trim fat from chops. Heat ½ teaspoon oil in a large nonstick skillet over medium-high heat. Add 3 chops; cook 3 minutes on each side or until browned. Repeat procedure with remaining oil and pork chops. Place chops over sauerkraut mixture in slow cooker. Pour reserved ¼ cup sauerkraut juice over pork.

3. Cover with lid; cook on high-heat setting 1 hour. Reduce to low-heat setting, and cook 5 hours or until pork is tender.

4. Prepare mashed potatoes according to package directions using 2⅓ cups fat-free milk. Serve chops and sauerkraut mixture over potatoes. Yield: 6 servings (serving size: about ¾ cup mashed potatoes, ⅔ cup sauerkraut mixture, and 1 pork chop).

Diabetic Exchanges: 1½ Starch, 1 Veg, 3 L Meat, ½ Sk Milk
Per serving: CAL 358 (28% from fat); PRO 30.9g; FAT 10.6g (sat 4.1g); CARB 31.8g; FIB 5.3g; CHOL 75mg; IRON 1.1mg; SOD 928mg; CALC 145mg

A bed of mashed potatoes absorbs the flavorful juices of Pork Chops with Sauerkraut and Caraway.

Enchilada Casserole

meatless main dishes

pepper in a bowl; stir well. Spoon batter evenly over bean mixture in slow cooker. Cover and cook 1 hour or until corn bread is done.

3. Sprinkle cheese over corn bread. Cover and cook 5 minutes or until cheese melts. Spoon casserole onto plates; top each serving with sour cream, and sprinkle with thinly sliced cilantro. Yield: 6 servings (serving size: about 1 cup casserole, 1 tablespoon sour cream, and ¼ teaspoon cilantro).

Diabetic Exchanges: 3 Starch, 1 Veg, 1 M-F Meat, 1 Fat
Per serving: CAL 385 (31% from fat); PRO 16.6g; FAT 13.0g (sat 5.9g); CARB 49.2g; FIB 5.1g; CHOL 23mg; IRON 3.0mg; SOD 1,129mg; CALC 344mg

Asparagus, Onion, and Mushroom Strata

Since the mixture chills overnight, you'll want to use a slow cooker with a removable crockery insert for this brunch recipe. The next morning, the strata is ready to slow cook while you visit with family or friends.

1 tablespoon olive oil
1 medium red onion, halved and thinly sliced (about 1½ cups)
1 cup sliced fresh mushrooms
Cooking spray
1 pound fresh asparagus spears
3 cups (½-inch) cubed French bread
½ cup (2 ounces) finely shredded fresh Parmigiano-Reggiano cheese, divided
1¼ cups 1% low-fat milk
1 cup egg substitute
¼ cup light mayonnaise
1 teaspoon salt
½ teaspoon white pepper
⅛ teaspoon ground cloves
½ cup (2 ounces) shredded reduced-fat sharp Cheddar cheese

1. Heat oil in a large nonstick skillet over medium-high heat. Add onion; sauté 10 minutes or until golden brown. Add mushrooms; sauté 5 minutes or until tender. Coat crockery insert of a 3½-quart electric slow cooker with cooking spray. Place onion mixture in insert.

2. Snap off tough ends of asparagus; remove scales with a knife or vegetable peeler, if desired.

Served with fresh fruit and warm bread, Asparagus, Onion, and Mushroom Strata is ideal for an informal gathering.

Enchilada Casserole ⊘

3 tablespoons diced green chiles, divided
½ cup salsa
¼ cup chopped green onions
¼ cup chopped fresh cilantro
1 (15-ounce) can black beans, rinsed and drained
1 (11-ounce) can corn with red and green peppers (such as Mexicorn), drained
1 (10-ounce) can enchilada sauce
1 (8½-ounce) package corn muffin mix
½ cup egg substitute
2 tablespoons chopped bottled roasted red bell pepper
1½ cups (6 ounces) shredded reduced-fat Monterey Jack cheese
6 tablespoons 30%-less-fat sour cream (such as Breakstone)
1½ teaspoons thinly sliced fresh cilantro

1. Place 2 tablespoons green chiles and next 6 ingredients in a 3½-quart electric slow cooker; stir well. Cover with lid; cook on low-heat setting 4 hours.

2. Combine remaining 1 tablespoon green chiles, muffin mix, egg substitute, and roasted bell

Cut each spear in half lengthwise; cut each half into 2-inch pieces. Add asparagus and bread to crockery insert; toss well. Sprinkle with ¼ cup Parmigiano-Reggiano cheese.

3. Combine milk and next 5 ingredients in a bowl; stir with a whisk until well blended. Pour milk mixture evenly over bread mixture; sprinkle with remaining Parmigiano-Reggiano cheese. Cover with lid; chill 8 hours or overnight.

4. Remove from refrigerator. Place crockery insert in slow cooker. Cook on high-heat setting 2½ to 3 hours. Sprinkle with Cheddar cheese; cover and cook 5 minutes or until cheese melts. Serve immediately. Yield: 6 servings (serving size: 1 cup).

Diabetic Exchanges: 1 Starch, 1 Veg, 1 V-L Meat, 1 M-F Meat, 1 Fat
Per serving: CAL 247 (40% from fat); PRO 17.0g; FAT 11.3g (sat 4.1g); CARB 20.6g; FIB 2.7g; CHOL 16mg; IRON 2.3mg; SOD 933mg; CALC 326mg

Parmesan, Spinach, and Barley Casserole

1   (32-ounce) container fat-free, less-sodium chicken broth (such as Swanson)
1   (16-ounce) can red beans, rinsed and drained
1   (8-ounce) package presliced fresh mushrooms
1½ cups uncooked fine barley
1½ cups sliced leek
1   cup chopped onion
1   teaspoon dried Italian seasoning
½   teaspoon pepper
½   teaspoon salt
1   (6-ounce) package fresh baby spinach
¾   cup (3 ounces) finely shredded fresh Parmesan cheese

1. Place first 9 ingredients in a 4-quart electric slow cooker; stir well. Cover with lid; cook on high-heat setting 3 hours. Add spinach. Cover and cook 15 minutes; stir well (spinach will wilt). Sprinkle each serving with cheese. Yield: 6 servings (serving size: 1½ cups casserole and 2 tablespoons cheese).

Diabetic Exchanges: 3 Starch, 1½ Veg, 1 L Meat
Per serving: CAL 313 (14% from fat); PRO 16.9g; FAT 4.8g (sat 2.7g); CARB 51.3g; FIB 6.4g; CHOL 11mg; IRON 3.3mg; SOD 949mg; CALC 262mg

Vegetable Paella

Reserve a little bit of oil from the jar of sun-dried tomatoes to add flavor to this meatless main dish.

2   cups uncooked converted rice (such as Uncle Ben's)
1   cup chopped onion
1   cup chopped green bell pepper
¼   cup chopped drained oil-packed sun-dried tomatoes
1½ tablespoons sun-dried tomato oil
1   teaspoon salt
1   (14½-ounce) can Mexican-style stewed tomatoes, undrained and chopped
1   (7.25-ounce) jar roasted red bell peppers, drained and chopped
4   garlic cloves, chopped
2   (14½-ounce) cans vegetable broth (such as Swanson)
1   (½-gram) package saffron threads (1 teaspoon)
1   (16-ounce) can chickpeas (garbanzo beans), rinsed and drained
1   (14-ounce) can quartered artichoke hearts, drained
1   cup frozen green peas

1. Place first 9 ingredients in a 3½- to 4-quart electric slow cooker; stir well. Combine broth and saffron. Add to slow cooker; stir well. Cover with lid; cook on low-heat setting 4 hours or until rice is tender and liquid is absorbed.

A twist on the traditional Spanish rice dish, Vegetable Paella showcases chickpeas and artichokes instead of sausage and shellfish.

2. Stir in chickpeas, artichoke hearts, and green peas. Cover and cook 15 minutes. Yield: 7 servings (serving size: 2 cups).

Diabetic Exchanges: 3½ Starch, 3 Veg, 1 Fat
Per serving: CAL 350 (14% from fat); PRO 9.8g; FAT 5.4g (sat 0.6g); CARB 66.7g; FIB 5.7g; CHOL 0mg; IRON 3.9mg; SOD 970mg; CALC 73mg

French Onion Soup

2   cups Caramelized Onions (page 80)
2   cups water
½   teaspoon dried thyme
1   (10½-ounce) can beef consommé
1   (10½-ounce) can condensed beef broth, undiluted
⅓   cup dry white wine
3   cups fat-free large-cut garlic-and-onion croutons
¾   cup (3 ounces) shredded reduced-fat Swiss cheese

1. Place Caramelized Onions, water, thyme, consommé, and broth in a 3½-quart electric slow cooker; stir well. Cover with lid; cook on high-heat setting 2½ hours or until thoroughly heated. Stir in wine.

2. Ladle 1 cup soup into each of 6 ovenproof bowls; top each with ½ cup croutons and 2 tablespoons Swiss cheese. Place bowls on a jelly-roll pan; broil 1 minute or until cheese melts. Yield: 6 servings.

Diabetic Exchanges: 1½ Starch, 1 Veg, ½ Fat
Per serving: CAL 215 (17% from fat); PRO 11.3g; FAT 3.7g (sat 2.2g); CARB 28.5g; FIB 1.4g; CHOL 14mg; IRON 0.6mg; SOD 984mg; CALC 154mg

Caponata with White Beans

4   cups (½-inch) cubed peeled eggplant
2   cups chopped tomato
1   cup chopped onion
1   cup chopped fennel bulb (about 1 medium)
½   cup raisins
⅓   cup chopped pimiento-stuffed green olives
3   tablespoons capers
1   tablespoon olive oil
1   tablespoon balsamic vinegar
¾   teaspoon salt
¼   teaspoon pepper
3   garlic cloves, minced

1   (15-ounce) can cannellini beans or other white beans, rinsed and drained
6¼ cups hot cooked rice, cooked without salt or fat

1. Place first 12 ingredients in a 3-quart electric slow cooker; toss gently. Cover with lid; cook on low-heat setting 6½ hours. Stir in beans; cover and cook 30 minutes or until eggplant is very tender. Serve over rice. Yield: 5 servings (serving size: 1 cup caponata and 1¼ cups rice).

Diabetic Exchanges: 4½ Starch, 3 Veg, ½ Fruit, ½ Fat
Per serving: CAL 442 (12% from fat); PRO 10.3g; FAT 5.8g (sat 0.9g); CARB 89.0g; FIB 8.5g; CHOL 0mg; IRON 4.6mg; SOD 849mg; CALC 80mg

Macaroni and Cheese ⊘

Cooking spray
¾   cup finely chopped onion
¾   cup finely chopped green bell pepper
3½ cups hot cooked elbow macaroni (about 1½ cups uncooked), cooked without salt or fat
1   tablespoon all-purpose flour
½   teaspoon dry mustard
⅛   teaspoon salt
⅛   teaspoon pepper
⅛   teaspoon ground red pepper
1½ cups 1% low-fat milk
1   cup (4 ounces) shredded reduced-fat sharp Cheddar cheese
2   ounces processed cheese, cubed (such as Velveeta)
1   (2-ounce) jar diced pimiento, drained

1. Coat a large nonstick skillet with cooking spray; place over medium-high heat until hot. Add onion and bell pepper; sauté 5 minutes or until tender. Place onion mixture and macaroni in a 3-quart electric slow cooker coated with cooking spray.

2. Place flour and next 4 ingredients in a small bowl; gradually add milk, stirring with a whisk until well blended. Add milk mixture, cheeses, and pimiento to slow cooker; stir well. Cover with lid; cook on high-heat setting 1½ hours or until thick and creamy, stirring after 1 hour. Yield: 4 servings (serving size: 1½ cups).

Diabetic Exchanges: 3 Starch, 1 Veg, 1 L Meat, ½ Sk Milk, 1 Fat
Per serving: CAL 356 (25% from fat); PRO 20.3g; FAT 9.8g (sat 5.8g); CARB 47.1g; FIB 2.9g; CHOL 25mg; IRON 2.3mg; SOD 538mg; CALC 451mg

Macaroni and Cheese

Barley, Black Bean, and Corn Burritos ⏱

1   (15-ounce) can black beans, rinsed and drained
1   (10-ounce) can diced tomatoes with green chiles, undrained
1   cup uncooked fine barley
2   cups fat-free, less-sodium chicken broth
¾   cup frozen whole-kernel corn
¼   cup chopped green onions
1   tablespoon fresh lime juice
1   teaspoon ground cumin
1   teaspoon chili powder
½   teaspoon cayenne pepper
1   garlic clove, minced
¼   cup chopped fresh cilantro
18 (6½-inch) flour tortillas
1   cup plus 2 tablespoons (4½ ounces) shredded reduced-fat sharp Cheddar cheese
9   cups thinly sliced curly leaf lettuce
2¼ cups salsa
1   cup plus 2 tablespoons fat-free sour cream

1. Place first 11 ingredients in a 3- to 4-quart electric slow cooker; stir well. Cover with lid; cook on low-heat setting 4 to 5 hours or until barley is tender and liquid is absorbed. Stir in cilantro.

Loaded with grains and vegetables, Barley, Black Bean, and Corn Burritos are a complete one-dish meal.

2. Heat tortillas according to package directions. Spoon ⅓ cup barley mixture down center of each tortilla; sprinkle each with 1 tablespoon cheese. Roll up. Place 1 cup lettuce on each of 9 plates; top each with 2 burritos. Spoon ¼ cup salsa and 2 tablespoons sour cream over each serving. Yield: 9 servings.

Diabetic Exchanges: 4 Starch, 1 Veg, ½ M-F Meat
Per serving: CAL 366 (11% from fat); PRO 17.6g; FAT 4.4g (sat 1.8g); CARB 65.5g; FIB 7.1g; CHOL 8mg; IRON 4.5mg; SOD 1,075mg; CALC 280mg

Curried Vegetables on Couscous

This high-flavor dish combines fresh vegetables with curry, cumin, cayenne, and chutney.

4   cups (½-inch) cubed peeled baking potato (about 1½ pounds)
4   cups cubed tomato (about 1½ pounds)
1   cup chopped onion
1   cup (¼-inch-thick) diagonally sliced carrot
2   tablespoons curry powder
2   teaspoons cumin seeds
1¼ teaspoons salt
¼   teaspoon cayenne pepper
2   (15-ounce) cans chickpeas (garbanzo beans), rinsed and drained
1   green bell pepper, cut into ½-inch-wide strips
3   garlic cloves, minced
⅓   cup chopped fresh cilantro
4   green onion tops, cut into 1-inch pieces
3   cups hot cooked couscous, cooked without salt or fat
6   tablespoons mango chutney
6   tablespoons raisins
6   tablespoons plain fat-free yogurt

1. Place potato in a 4-quart electric slow cooker. Combine tomato and next 9 ingredients in a bowl; stir well. Spoon over potato. Cover with lid; cook on low-heat setting 9 hours. Stir in cilantro and green onions. Serve over couscous; top with chutney, raisins, and yogurt. Yield: 6 servings (serving size: 1⅔ cups vegetables, ½ cup couscous, 1 tablespoon chutney, 1 tablespoon raisins, and 1 tablespoon yogurt).

Diabetic Exchanges: 4 Starch, 3 Veg, ½ Fruit
Per serving: CAL 377 (5% from fat); PRO 12.0g; FAT 2.2g (sat 0.3g); CARB 81.1g; FIB 11.0g; CHOL 0mg; IRON 3.9mg; SOD 767mg; CALC 101mg

Chili-Cheese Spuds

4   (6-ounce) baking potatoes
1   (15-ounce) can vegetarian chili with beans
½   cup (2 ounces) finely shredded Cheddar
    cheese
¼   cup 30%-less-fat sour cream (such as
    Breakstone)
¼   cup sliced green onions

1. Scrub potatoes; shake to remove excess moisture (do not dry potatoes). Place wet potatoes in a
4- to 5-quart electric slow cooker. Cover with lid;
cook on low-heat setting 10 hours or until potatoes are tender.

2. Heat chili according to package directions.
Split open each potato; fluff pulp with a fork.
Spoon about ½ cup chili into center of each
potato; top each potato with 2 tablespoons
cheese, 1 tablespoon sour cream, and 1 tablespoon green onions. Yield: 4 servings.

Diabetic Exchanges: 3½ Starch, 1 V-L Meat, 1 Fat
Per serving: CAL 322 (19% from fat); PRO 12.5g; FAT 7.0g (sat
4.3g); CARB 52.8g; FIB 7.8g; CHOL 23mg; IRON 3.5mg; SOD
444mg; CALC 182mg

Eggplant and Artichoke Parmigiana ⏱

Get a jump start on this recipe by assembling the
ingredients in the crockery insert the night before
you plan to serve it. The next day it can go
straight from the fridge to the slow cooker; sim-
ply add about one hour to the total cook time to
compensate for the chilled ingredients.

1   (25-ounce) jar roasted garlic pasta sauce with
    Merlot wine (such as Sutter Home), divided
½   teaspoon freshly ground pepper
1   (1-pound) eggplant, cut into ¼-inch-thick
    slices
1   (9-ounce) package frozen artichoke hearts,
    thawed and drained
1   cup (4 ounces) shredded part-skim
    mozzarella cheese
2   tablespoons chopped fresh flat-leaf parsley
1   tablespoon chopped fresh oregano
4   cups hot cooked thin spaghetti (about 8
    ounces uncooked pasta), cooked without salt
    or fat
¼   cup finely shredded fresh Parmigiano-
    Reggiano cheese or Parmesan cheese

1. Combine pasta sauce and pepper; stir well.
Spoon ½ cup pasta sauce into a 4-quart electric
slow cooker. Arrange half of eggplant slices over
sauce; top with half of artichoke hearts, and
sprinkle with half of mozzarella cheese. Spoon ½
cup pasta sauce over mozzarella cheese.

2. Repeat layers with remaining eggplant slices,
artichoke hearts, and mozzarella cheese. Top with
remaining pasta sauce; sprinkle with chopped
parsley and chopped oregano. Cover with lid;
cook on low-heat setting 5 to 6 hours or until
eggplant is tender. Serve eggplant mixture over
pasta; sprinkle with fresh Parmigiano-Reggiano
cheese. Yield: 4 servings (serving size: about 1½
cups Parmigiana, 1 cup pasta, and 1 tablespoon
Parmigiano-Reggiano cheese).

Diabetic Exchanges: 3 Starch, 5 Veg, 1 M-F Meat, 1 Fat
Per serving: CAL 461 (21% from fat); PRO 22.6g; FAT 11.1g (sat
4.5g); CARB 68.9g; FIB 17.6g; CHOL 20mg; IRON 3.4mg; SOD
996mg; CALC 358mg

**Eggplant and Artichoke
Parmigiana is a cinch to
make. We skipped breading
and frying the eggplant
and started with a bottled
pasta sauce.**

Maple-Hazelnut Oatmeal

Maple-Hazelnut Oatmeal

1½ cups fat-free milk
1½ cups water
2   Gala apples, peeled, cored, and cut into
    ½-inch cubes (about 3 cups)
1   cup uncooked steel-cut oats (such as
    McCann's Irish Oatmeal)
2   tablespoons brown sugar
1½ tablespoons butter or stick margarine,
    softened
¼   teaspoon ground cinnamon
¼   teaspoon salt
Cooking spray
¼   cup real maple syrup
2   tablespoons chopped hazelnuts, toasted

1. Bring milk and water to a boil in a saucepan over medium-high heat, stirring frequently.

2. Place hot milk mixture, apple, and next 5 ingredients in a 3½-quart electric slow cooker coated with cooking spray; stir well. Cover with lid; cook on low-heat setting 7 hours or until oats are tender.

3. Spoon oatmeal into bowls; top with maple syrup and hazelnuts. Yield: 4 servings (serving size: 1¼ cups oatmeal, 1 tablespoon syrup, and 1½ teaspoons hazelnuts).

Diabetic Exchanges: 3 Starch, 1 Fruit, 1 Fat
Per serving: CAL 363 (23% from fat); PRO 9.3g; FAT 9.7g (sat 3.4g); CARB 63.8g; FIB 5.6g; CHOL 13mg; IRON 2.5mg; SOD 242mg; CALC 161mg

Cheesy Barley-Lentil Casserole ⊗

5   cups water
3   vegetarian vegetable bouillon cubes (such
    as Knorr's)
1   (8-ounce) package presliced fresh
    mushrooms
1   cup uncooked fine barley
1   cup dried brown lentils
1   cup chopped carrot
¾   cup chopped onion
½   cup chopped green bell pepper
½   teaspoon dried thyme
¼   teaspoon pepper
1   bay leaf
1   cup (4 ounces) shredded reduced-fat sharp
    Cheddar cheese, divided
3   tablespoons unsalted sunflower seeds

1. Combine water and bouillon cubes in a saucepan; bring to a boil, stirring until cubes

dissolve. Pour into a 4-quart electric slow cooker; stir in mushrooms, barley, lentils, carrot, onion, bell pepper, thyme, pepper, and bay leaf. Cover with lid; cook on low-heat setting 6 hours or until barley is tender and liquid is absorbed. Discard bay leaf. Stir in ½ cup cheese. Spoon barley mixture into bowls; sprinkle with remaining cheese and sunflower seeds. Yield: 9 servings (serving size: 1 cup barley mixture, about 2½ teaspoons cheese, and 1 teaspoon sunflower seeds).

Diabetic Exchanges: 2 Starch, ½ Veg, 1 V-L Meat, ½ Fat
Per serving: CAL 216 (19% from fat); PRO 12.0g; FAT 4.7g (sat 1.9g); CARB 32.0g; FIB 6.8g; CHOL 5mg; IRON 2.7mg; SOD 671mg; CALC 135mg

Mexican Black-Bean Chili

If you prefer, skip the first step of this recipe and soak the beans overnight.

1   pound dried black beans
2   cups water
2   cups chopped onion
1   cup coarsely chopped yellow bell pepper
1   cup coarsely chopped red bell pepper
1   cup coarsely chopped green bell pepper
¼   cup semisweet chocolate chips
2   tablespoons chopped seeded jalapeño
    pepper
2   teaspoons chili powder
1½ teaspoons dried oregano
1   teaspoon ground cumin
2   teaspoons hot sauce
½   teaspoon ground cinnamon
4   garlic cloves, minced
2   (14½-ounce) cans chili-style chunky
    tomatoes, undrained
1   (6-ounce) can tomato paste
¼   teaspoon salt
6   tablespoons (1½ ounces) shredded
    Monterey Jack cheese
6   tablespoons 30%-less-fat sour cream (such
    as Breakstone)
2   tablespoons minced fresh cilantro

1. Sort and wash beans; place in a large Dutch oven. Cover with water to 2 inches above beans; bring to a boil, and cook 2 minutes. Remove from heat; cover and let stand 1 hour. Drain beans.

2. Place beans, 2 cups water, onion, bell peppers, chocolate chips, and next 7 ingredients in a

4-quart electric slow cooker; stir well. Cover with lid; cook on low-heat setting 8 to 9 hours or until beans are tender. Stir in tomatoes, tomato paste, and salt. Ladle chili into bowls; top each serving with cheese, sour cream, and cilantro. Yield: 6 servings (serving size: 1¾ cups chili, 1 tablespoon cheese, 1 tablespoon sour cream, and 1 teaspoon cilantro).

Diabetic Exchanges: 4 Starch, 3½ Veg, 1 V-L Meat, 1 Fat
Per serving: CAL 449 (15% from fat); PRO 23.5g; FAT 7.7g (sat 4.1g); CARB 77.5g; FIB 18.1g; CHOL 14mg; IRON 6.1mg; SOD 937mg; CALC 229mg

Hoppin' John ⊘

2   (16-ounce) packages frozen black-eyed peas
1¼ cups sliced green onions, divided
2   cups hot water
¾   cup chopped red bell pepper
2   tablespoons minced seeded jalapeño
      pepper
2   teaspoons hot sauce
½   teaspoon salt
¼   teaspoon pepper
1   chicken-flavored bouillon cube
1   (14½-ounce) can Cajun stewed tomatoes, undrained
⅔   cup uncooked converted rice (such as Uncle Ben's)

1. Place peas, ¾ cup green onions, water, and next 6 ingredients in a 4-quart electric slow cooker; stir well. Cover with lid; cook on high-heat setting 4 hours. Stir in tomatoes and rice; cover and cook 1 hour or until peas and rice are tender and most of liquid is absorbed. Stir in remaining ½ cup green onions. Yield: 6 servings (serving size: 1⅔ cups).

Diabetic Exchanges: 3½ Starch, 1 Veg, 1 V-L Meat
Per serving: CAL 307 (3% from fat); PRO 15.0g; FAT 1.2g (sat 0.3g); CARB 60.2g; FIB 12.1g; CHOL 0mg; IRON 4.2mg; SOD 651mg; CALC 60mg

Introduced to the South by African slaves, Hoppin' John is said to bring good luck all year when eaten on New Year's Day.

Black Bean and Rice Stuffed Peppers ⏱

These peppers get buttery soft without blanching.

2   cups water
1   (8-ounce) package uncooked seasoned black bean-and-rice mix
4   large green bell peppers (about 1¾ pounds)
1   cup (4 ounces) shredded Cheddar-Jack cheese
1   (10-ounce) can diced tomatoes with green chiles, undrained
1   (8¾-ounce) can no-salt-added whole-kernel corn, drained
1   (2¼-ounce) can sliced ripe olives, drained
1   (12-ounce) bottle Mexican amber lager beer (such as Dos Equis)
1   (6-ounce) can no-salt-added tomato paste

1. Bring 2 cups water to a boil in a saucepan; stir in bean-and-rice mix. Return to a boil, and cook 1 minute, stirring constantly. Cover, reduce heat, and simmer 12 minutes or until water is absorbed (beans and rice will still be crunchy), stirring after 6 minutes. Remove bean-and-rice mix from heat; set aside.

2. Cut tops off bell peppers; discard stems. Chop pepper tops to measure 1 cup. Remove seeds and membranes from peppers; discard. Combine bean-and-rice mix, 1 cup chopped bell pepper, cheese, and next 3 ingredients in a bowl; stir well. Spoon mixture evenly into bell peppers. Place stuffed peppers, upright, in a 4-quart electric slow cooker.

3. Combine beer and tomato paste in a small bowl, stirring with a whisk until well blended. Pour beer mixture over tops of stuffed peppers. Cover with lid; cook on high-heat setting 1 hour. Reduce to low-heat setting, and cook 2 to 3 hours or until beans and rice are tender. Serve tomato sauce mixture with stuffed peppers. Yield: 4 servings (serving size: 1 stuffed pepper and about ⅓ cup sauce).

Diabetic Exchanges: 4 Starch, 3 Veg, 1 M-F Meat, ½ Fat
Per serving: CAL 455 (22% from fat); PRO 18.6g; FAT 11.6g (sat 6.1g); CARB 76.3g; FIB 11.6g; CHOL 27mg; IRON 3.9mg; SOD 1,268mg; CALC 313mg

Vegetable Soup ⏱

1   (16-ounce) package frozen whole-kernel corn, thawed and drained
1   (16-ounce) package frozen baby lima beans, thawed and drained
2   (14½-ounce) cans diced tomatoes with basil, garlic, and oregano, undrained
2   (14½-ounce) cans vegetable broth (such as Swanson)
1   (10-ounce) package frozen sliced okra, thawed and drained
1¼ cups chopped onion
2   teaspoons hot sauce
2   teaspoons Worcestershire sauce
¾   teaspoon salt
½   teaspoon dried thyme
½   teaspoon freshly ground pepper
3   garlic cloves, minced
1   bay leaf

1. Place all ingredients in a 4-quart electric slow cooker; stir well. Cover with lid; cook on high-heat setting 5 to 6 hours or until vegetables are tender. Yield: 8 servings (serving size: 1¼ cups).

Diabetic Exchanges: 1½ Starch, 3 Veg
Per serving: CAL 185 (5% from fat); PRO 9.2g; FAT 1.2g (sat 0.1g); CARB 38.9g; FIB 7.1g; CHOL 0mg; IRON 3.3mg; SOD 1,049mg; CALC 122mg

Black Bean and Rice Stuffed Peppers simmer in a beer-spiked tomato sauce for a robust flavor.

Chickpeas in Curried Coconut Broth ⊙

2   teaspoons canola or vegetable oil
1½ cups chopped onion
2   garlic cloves, minced
2   (19-ounce) cans chickpeas (garbanzo beans), rinsed and drained
2   (14½-ounce) cans diced tomatoes, undrained
1   (14-ounce) can coconut milk
1   tablespoon curry powder
2   tablespoons chopped pickled jalapeño pepper
1½ teaspoons salt
½   cup chopped fresh cilantro
6   cups hot cooked basmati rice, cooked without salt or fat

1. Heat oil in a large nonstick skillet over medium heat. Add onion and garlic; sauté 5 minutes or until onion is tender. Place onion mixture, chickpeas, tomatoes, coconut milk, curry powder, jalapeño pepper, and salt in a 3½-quart electric slow cooker; stir well. Cover with lid; cook on low-heat setting 6 to 8 hours. Stir in cilantro. Serve over rice. Yield: 8 servings (serving size: 1 cup chickpea mixture and ¾ cup rice).

Diabetic Exchanges: 4 Starch, 1 Veg, 2 Fat
Per serving: CAL 404 (30% from fat); PRO 9.0g; FAT 13.8g (sat 9.5g); CARB 62.9g; FIB 7.6g; CHOL 0mg; IRON 5.3mg; SOD 670mg; CALC 63mg

Cuban Rice and Red Beans ⊙

2   teaspoons vegetable oil
1½ cups chopped green bell pepper
1   cup chopped onion
3   garlic cloves, minced
2   (16-ounce) cans light red kidney beans, drained and rinsed
1   (10-ounce) can diced tomatoes with green chiles, undrained
2   cups water
1   teaspoon salt
1   teaspoon ground cumin
½   teaspoon dried oregano
¼   teaspoon black pepper
¼   teaspoon cayenne pepper
4   cups hot cooked converted rice (such as Uncle Ben's), cooked without salt or fat
⅓   cup chopped fresh cilantro
2   tablespoons fresh lime juice

1. Heat oil in a large nonstick skillet over medium-high heat. Add bell pepper and onion; sauté 5 minutes or until tender. Add garlic; sauté 1 minute. Place bell pepper mixture in a 5-quart electric slow cooker. Add beans, tomatoes, water, salt, cumin, oregano, black pepper, and cayenne pepper; stir well. Cover with lid; cook on low-heat setting 4 hours. Stir in remaining ingredients. Yield: 5 servings (serving size: 1½ cups).

Diabetic Exchanges: 3½ Starch, 2 Veg, ½ Fat
Per serving: CAL 312 (8% from fat); PRO 10.7g; FAT 2.9g (sat 0.3g); CARB 61.4g; FIB 9.4g; CHOL 0mg; IRON 3.7mg; SOD 813mg; CALC 78mg

Homestyle Potato Soup ⊙

1   (14½-ounce) can fat-free, less-sodium chicken broth
4   cups cubed peeled baking potato (about 2 pounds)
1   cup chopped onion
1   cup thinly sliced celery
¾   cup thinly sliced carrot
3   tablespoons butter or stick margarine, cut into small pieces
1¼ teaspoons salt
½   teaspoon freshly ground pepper
3   garlic cloves, minced
¼   cup all-purpose flour
1½ cups 2% reduced-fat milk
7   tablespoons (1¾ ounces) shredded reduced-fat sharp Cheddar cheese
Freshly ground pepper (optional)

1. Place first 9 ingredients in a 4½-quart electric slow cooker; stir well. Cover with lid; cook on high-heat setting 1 hour. Reduce to low-heat setting, and cook 4 to 5 hours or until vegetables are tender. Increase to high-heat setting.
2. Place flour in a bowl; gradually add milk, stirring with a whisk until well blended. Stir into soup. Cook, uncovered, 25 minutes or until thick, stirring frequently. Ladle into bowls; sprinkle with cheese. Sprinkle with pepper, if desired. Yield: 7 servings (serving size: 1 cup soup and 1 tablespoon cheese).

Diabetic Exchanges: 2 Starch, 1 Veg, 1 Fat
Per serving: CAL 238 (27% from fat); PRO 7.9g; FAT 7.3g (sat 4.5g); CARB 36.5g; FIB 3.5g; CHOL 20mg; IRON 0.9mg; SOD 727mg; CALC 156mg

Homestyle Potato Soup

other meats

Thai Coconut Shrimp and Rice

Osso Buco

Thai Coconut Shrimp and Rice ⏱

2   cups red bell pepper strips
2   cups fat-free, less-sodium chicken broth
1½ cups uncooked converted rice (such as Uncle Ben's)
½   cup thinly sliced peeled carrot
1½ teaspoons Thai chili garlic paste
2   (8-ounce) bottles clam juice
1   (14-ounce) can light coconut milk
10 (⅛-inch-thick) slices peeled fresh ginger
5   garlic cloves, minced
1½ pounds large shrimp, peeled
2   cups fresh sugar snap peas, trimmed
½   cup (1-inch) sliced green onion tops
⅓   cup fresh lime juice
⅛   teaspoon salt
¼   cup flaked sweetened coconut, toasted

1. Place first 9 ingredients in a 4-quart electric slow cooker; stir well. Cover with lid; cook on low-heat setting 4 hours.

2. Increase to high-heat setting. Add shrimp and next 4 ingredients; cover and cook 30 minutes or until shrimp are done. Spoon into bowls; sprinkle with coconut. Yield: 6 servings (serving size: 2 cups rice mixture and 2 teaspoons coconut).

Diabetic Exchanges: 3 Starch, 2 Veg, 2 V-L Meat, 1 Fat
Per serving: CAL 372 (14% from fat); PRO 21.8g; FAT 5.6g (sat 3.4g); CARB 57.3g; FIB 4.1g; CHOL 137mg; IRON 5.3mg; SOD 726mg; CALC 112mg

Osso Buco

2   tablespoons all-purpose flour
¾   teaspoon pepper
4   (10-ounce) veal shanks (1½ inches thick)
1   tablespoon olive oil
1   cup chopped carrot
1   cup chopped celery
1   cup chopped onion
1   large garlic clove, minced
½   cup dry white wine
1   (14.5-ounce) can diced tomatoes, drained
1   tablespoon chopped fresh rosemary
½   teaspoon salt
1   bay leaf
Rosemary sprigs (optional)

1. Combine flour and pepper in a pie plate or shallow dish; stir well. Dredge veal in flour mixture; set aside.

2. Heat oil in a large nonstick skillet over medium-high heat. Add veal; cook 2 minutes on each side or until browned. Place veal in a 4-quart electric slow cooker; set aside.

3. Add carrot and next 3 ingredients to skillet; sauté over medium heat 5 minutes. Add wine, scraping bottom of skillet to loosen browned bits. Cook 1 minute. Pour vegetable mixture over veal in slow cooker. Add tomatoes, rosemary, salt, and bay leaf. Cover with lid; cook on high-heat setting 1 hour. Reduce to low-heat setting, and cook 6 to 7 hours or until veal is tender. Discard bay leaf. Garnish with rosemary sprigs, if desired. Yield: 4 servings (serving size: 1 veal shank and 1¼ cups sauce).

Diabetic Exchanges: 3 Veg, 6 L Meat
Per serving: CAL 328 (22% from fat); PRO 48.3g; FAT 7.6g (sat 1.8g); CARB 14.6g; FIB 3.0g; CHOL 180mg; IRON 2.9mg; SOD 638mg; CALC 103mg

Venison Swiss Steak

Fines herbes, a mixture of chervil, chives, parsley, and tarragon, adds complex flavor notes to this venison dish.

2   pounds venison steak or beef round steak
¼   teaspoon paprika
¼   teaspoon pepper
1   tablespoon olive oil, divided
1½ cups chopped onion
1   (14½-ounce) can diced tomatoes, undrained
1   (1-ounce) envelope onion soup mix
½   cup dry red wine
¼   teaspoon fines herbes
1   tablespoon cornstarch
2   tablespoons water

1. Trim fat from venison. Place venison between 2 sheets of heavy-duty plastic wrap; flatten to a ½-inch thickness using a meat mallet or rolling pin. Cut into 8 equal portions; sprinkle paprika and pepper evenly over both sides of steaks.

2. Heat 1 teaspoon oil in a large nonstick skillet over medium-high heat. Add 3 steaks; cook until browned on both sides. Place browned steaks in a 4-quart electric slow cooker. Repeat procedure twice with remaining oil and steaks. Add onion to skillet; sauté 5 minutes or until tender. Add tomatoes, soup mix, wine, and fines herbes; stir well. Bring to a boil, and pour over steaks in slow cooker. Cover with lid; cook on high-heat setting 1 hour. Reduce to low-heat setting, and cook 6 to 8 hours or until steaks are tender.

3. Place steaks on a serving platter, reserving tomato mixture in slow cooker. Set steaks aside, and keep warm. Increase to high-heat setting. Combine cornstarch and water in a small bowl; stir until well blended. Stir cornstarch mixture into tomato mixture. Cook, uncovered, until slightly thick, stirring frequently. Pour tomato mixture over steaks. Yield: 8 servings (serving size: 3 ounces venison and about ⅓ cup sauce).

Diabetic Exchanges: 1 Veg, 3½ V-L Meat
Per serving: CAL 188 (23% from fat); PRO 27.3g; FAT 4.7g (sat 1.4g); CARB 8.1g; FIB 1.8g; CHOL 97mg; IRON 4.2mg; SOD 443mg; CALC 26mg

A slow cooker and our recipe for Ragoût of Veal take the stress out of casual entertaining.

Ragoût of Veal ☉

1   (2½-pound) lean boneless veal tip round roast
1½ teaspoons paprika
¾ teaspoon freshly ground pepper
½ teaspoon salt
Cooking spray
1   tablespoon olive oil, divided
½ cup dry white wine
3   cups sliced leeks (about 3 large)
3   garlic cloves, minced
⅓ cup all-purpose flour
1   (14½-ounce) can chicken broth
3   cups (½-inch) sliced peeled carrot
5   thyme sprigs
1   bay leaf
8   cups hot cooked fettuccine (about 16 ounces uncooked pasta), cooked without salt or fat
2   tablespoons chopped fresh flat-leaf parsley

1. Trim fat from veal; cut veal into 1-inch cubes. Sprinkle paprika, pepper, and salt over veal.
2. Coat a large nonstick skillet with cooking spray; add 1 teaspoon oil, and place over medium-high heat until hot. Add half of veal; sauté 4 minutes until browned. Place browned veal in a 6-quart electric slow cooker. Repeat procedure with 1 teaspoon oil and remaining veal. Add wine to skillet; cook 1 minute, scraping skillet to loosen browned bits. Pour over veal in slow cooker.
3. Heat remaining 1 teaspoon oil in skillet over medium-high heat. Add leeks and garlic; sauté 3 minutes. Spoon leek mixture over veal in slow cooker.
4. Place flour in a small bowl; gradually add broth, stirring until well blended. Pour broth mixture into slow cooker. Add carrot, thyme, and bay leaf; stir well. Cover with lid; cook on high-heat setting 1 hour. Reduce to low-heat setting; cook 3 hours or until veal is tender. Discard thyme sprigs and bay leaf. Serve veal mixture over fettuccine; sprinkle with parsley. Yield: 8 servings (serving size: 1 cup veal ragoût, 1 cup pasta, and ¾ teaspoon parsley).

Diabetic Exchanges: 3 Starch, 2 Veg, 3 V-L Meat, 1 Fat
Per serving: CAL 439 (18% from fat); PRO 33.7g; FAT 8.8g (sat 2.7g); CARB 54.8g; FIB 4.8g; CHOL 97mg; IRON 4.3mg; SOD 406mg; CALC 71mg

Aegean Lamb with Orzo

When purchasing a leg of lamb, tell the butcher that you want it "boned, rolled, and tied." The butcher will debone the leg, roll it up into a whole roast, and secure it with butcher twine.

3½ pounds lean rolled boneless leg of lamb
¼ cup chopped fresh oregano
2 teaspoons grated lemon rind
¾ teaspoon salt, divided
¼ cup fresh lemon juice
1 (10-ounce) bag fresh spinach, chopped
5½ cups hot cooked orzo (about 2½ cups uncooked rice-shaped pasta), cooked without salt or fat
1 cup (4 ounces) crumbled feta cheese
Oregano sprigs (optional)
Lemon slices (optional)

1. Unroll roast, and trim fat. Reroll roast, and secure with twine. Cut roast in half crosswise. Place roast halves in a 4½- to 5-quart electric slow cooker; sprinkle with oregano, lemon rind, and ¼ teaspoon salt. Drizzle with lemon juice. Cover with lid; cook on high-heat setting 1 hour. Reduce to low-heat setting, and cook 7 hours or until lamb is tender. Add spinach to slow cooker. Cover and cook on low-heat setting 15 minutes. Remove spinach and lamb from slow cooker, reserving cooking liquid. Remove twine from roast halves, and chop roast.

2. Pour cooking liquid into a bowl; let stand 5 minutes. Skim fat from surface of liquid.

3. Add remaining ½ teaspoon salt, chopped lamb, spinach, orzo, and feta to cooking liquid; toss well. Garnish with oregano sprigs and lemon slices, if desired. Yield: 10 servings (serving size: 1 cup).

Diabetic Exchanges: 2½ Starch, 4 L Meat, ½ M-F Meat
Per serving: CAL 414 (25% from fat); PRO 36.2g; FAT 11.5g (sat 5.0g); CARB 39.5g; FIB 1.5g; CHOL 98mg; IRON 4.8mg; SOD 432mg; CALC 127mg

Venison with Stout and Potatoes

1 (2-pound) venison steak
4 cups cubed red potato (about 1½ pounds)
1¼ teaspoons salt
1 teaspoon pepper
2 cups chopped onion
¼ cup all-purpose flour
1 (12-ounce) bottle stout beer
2 tablespoons Dijon mustard
2 bay leaves
1 (8-ounce) package presliced fresh mushrooms
1 tablespoon fresh thyme leaves

1. Trim fat from venison; cut venison into 1-inch cubes. Place a large nonstick skillet over medium-high heat until hot. Add venison; sauté until browned. Place venison in a 3½-quart electric slow cooker. Add potato to slow cooker; sprinkle with salt and pepper.

2. Add onion to skillet; sauté over medium-high heat 3 minutes or until lightly browned. Stir in flour; cook 1 minute. Gradually add beer, stirring until well blended. Stir in Dijon mustard. Add beer mixture and bay leaves to slow cooker. Cover with lid; cook on high-heat setting 1 hour. Reduce to low-heat setting, and cook 4 hours. Stir in mushrooms. Cover and cook on low-heat setting 2 hours. Discard bay leaves. Stir in thyme just before serving. Yield: 6 servings (serving size: 1⅓ cups).

Diabetic Exchanges: 2 Starch, 1 Veg, 4½ V-L Meat
Per serving: CAL 348 (12% from fat); PRO 39.7g; FAT 4.5g (sat 1.5g); CARB 36.4g; FIB 3.9g; CHOL 129mg; IRON 7.3mg; SOD 606mg; CALC 46mg

With a combination of feta cheese, spinach, oregano, and lemon, Aegean Lamb with Orzo brings the Greek Isles to your table.

minute, stirring frequently. Remove from heat; stir in tomatoes, parsley, salt, oregano, black pepper, and red pepper.

2. Place roast in a 5-quart electric slow cooker; pour tomato mixture over roast. Cover with lid; cook on high-heat setting 1 hour. Reduce to low-heat setting, and cook 7 to 9 hours or until tender. Remove roast from slow cooker, reserving sauce. Slice roast; keep warm.

3. Bring 6 cups water to a boil in a large saucepan. Stir in grits and ¾ teaspoon salt; return to a boil. Cover, reduce heat, and simmer 5 minutes or until thick, stirring occasionally. Serve venison and sauce over grits. Yield: 6 servings (serving size: 1 cup grits, 3 ounces venison, and ½ cup sauce).

Diabetic Exchanges: 2½ Starch, 1 Veg, 3 V-L Meat, 1 Fat
Per serving: CAL 360 (20% from fat); PRO 29.2g; FAT 7.7g (sat 1.7g); CARB 42.4g; FIB 2.5g; CHOL 90mg; IRON 5.8mg; SOD 821mg; CALC 29mg

Veal Paprikash

1 (2¼-pound) lean boneless veal tip round roast
1 (8-ounce) package presliced fresh mushrooms
1½ cups sliced carrot
1 cup slivered onion
2 tablespoons chopped fresh parsley
4 garlic cloves, minced
2 bay leaves
¼ cup all-purpose flour
1 tablespoon Hungarian sweet paprika
¾ teaspoon salt
½ teaspoon dried thyme
½ teaspoon pepper
¼ cup dry white wine
½ cup 30%-less-fat sour cream (such as Breakstone)
5¼ cups hot cooked medium egg noodles (about 10 ounces uncooked), cooked without salt or fat
3½ teaspoons chopped fresh parsley
7 teaspoons chopped fresh chives

1. Trim fat from veal; cut veal into 1-inch cubes. Place veal and next 6 ingredients in a 3½-quart electric slow cooker; toss well. Combine flour,

Drenched in a rich sauce, Venison Grillade and Grits offers plenty of Creole flavor.

Venison Grillade and Grits

2 tablespoons all-purpose flour
2 tablespoons vegetable oil
1 cup chopped onion
½ cup chopped green bell pepper
3 garlic cloves, minced
1 (14½-ounce) can diced tomatoes, undrained
1 tablespoon chopped fresh parsley
1 teaspoon salt
½ teaspoon dried oregano
¼ teaspoon black pepper
¼ teaspoon ground red pepper
1 (2-pound) boneless venison roast
6 cups water
1½ cups quick-cooking grits
¾ teaspoon salt

1. Place flour in a small skillet; gradually add oil, stirring with a whisk until well blended. Place over medium heat, and cook 8 minutes or until golden. Add onion and bell pepper; cook 5 minutes, stirring frequently. Add garlic, and cook 1

paprika, salt, thyme, and pepper in a small bowl; gradually add wine, stirring until well blended. Add flour mixture to slow cooker; stir well. Cover with lid; cook on high-heat setting 1 hour. Reduce to low-heat setting, and cook 6 hours or until veal and vegetables are tender. Discard bay leaves.

2. Turn slow cooker off, and let mixture stand 5 minutes. Stir in sour cream. Serve veal mixture over egg noodles; sprinkle with parsley and chives. Yield: 7 servings (serving size: ¾ cup veal mixture, ¾ cup egg noodles, ½ teaspoon parsley, and 1 teaspoon chives).

Diabetic Exchanges: 2½ Starch, 1 Veg, 4 V-L Meat, 1 Fat
Per serving: CAL 392 (20% from fat); PRO 35.7g; FAT 8.6g (sat 3.1g); CARB 42.1g; FIB 3.5g; CHOL 152mg; IRON 4.2mg; SOD 328mg; CALC 92mg

Cioppino

1 tablespoon olive oil
2 cups chopped onion
1½ cups chopped celery
1½ cups diced green bell pepper
4 garlic cloves, minced
2 (10-ounce) cans diced tomatoes with green chiles, undrained
1 (8-ounce) bottle clam juice
1 (6-ounce) can tomato paste
1 cup dry white wine
3 tablespoons red wine vinegar
1 teaspoon dried thyme
¼ teaspoon crushed red pepper
1¼ pounds little neck clams (about 24), scrubbed
1 pound large shrimp, peeled
½ pound grouper or other firm white fish fillet, cut into 1-inch cubes
½ pound lump crabmeat, drained and shell pieces removed
Thyme sprigs (optional)

1. Heat oil in a large nonstick skillet over medium-high heat. Add onion and next 3 ingredients; sauté 6 minutes or until vegetables are tender. Place onion mixture in a 4½-quart electric slow cooker. Add tomatoes and next 6 ingredients; stir well. Cover with lid; cook on low-heat setting 6 hours.

2. Increase to high-heat setting. Add clams; cover and cook 20 minutes. Add shrimp, grouper, and crabmeat; cover and cook 10 to 15 minutes or until clams open and fish flakes easily when tested with a fork. Discard any unopened shells. Garnish with thyme sprigs, if desired. Yield: 6 servings (serving size: 1¾ cups).

Diabetic Exchanges: ½ Starch, 2 Veg, 4 V-L Meat
Per serving: CAL 259 (16% from fat); PRO 34.9g; FAT 4.6g (sat 0.7g); CARB 19.4g; FIB 4.6g; CHOL 162mg; IRON 11.6mg; SOD 809mg; CALC 148mg

Tarragon Lamb Shanks with Cannellini Beans

4 (1½-pound) lamb shanks
1 (19-ounce) can cannellini beans or other white beans, rinsed and drained
1½ cups diced peeled carrot
1 cup chopped onion
¾ cup chopped celery
2 garlic cloves, thinly sliced
2 teaspoons dried tarragon

Created by San Francisco's Italian immigrants, Cioppino is a flavorful stew made with tomatoes and a variety of fish and shellfish.

½ teaspoon salt
¼ teaspoon pepper
1 (28-ounce) can diced tomatoes, undrained

1. Trim fat from lamb shanks. Place beans and next 4 ingredients in a 4- to 6-quart electric slow cooker; stir well. Place lamb shanks on bean mixture; sprinkle with tarragon, salt, and pepper. Pour tomatoes over lamb. Cover with lid; cook on high-heat setting 1 hour. Reduce to low-heat setting, and cook 9 hours or until lamb is very tender.

2. Remove lamb shanks from slow cooker. Pour bean mixture through a colander or sieve over a bowl, reserving liquid. Let liquid stand 5 minutes; skim fat from surface of liquid. Return bean mixture to liquid. Remove lamb from bones, and serve with bean mixture. Yield: 12 servings (serving size: about 3 ounces lamb and ⅔ cup bean mixture).

Diabetic Exchanges: ½ Starch, 1 Veg, 3 L Meat
Per serving: CAL 226 (39% from fat); PRO 22.4g; FAT 9.7g (sat 3.9g); CARB 11.4g; FIB 3.3g; CHOL 68mg; IRON 2.4mg; SOD 296mg; CALC 43mg

Curry Stew with Lamb

Thai seasoning and dried lemon grass are available in the spice section of most large supermarkets. Fish sauce can be found on the ethnic aisle or in Asian markets. All three ingredients add distinctive flavor to this dish.

1½ pounds lean boneless leg of lamb
¼ cup firmly packed fresh basil leaves
1 tablespoon Thai seasoning (such as McCormick)
3 tablespoons chopped peeled fresh ginger
3 tablespoons fresh lime juice
2 teaspoons curry powder
1 teaspoon dried lemon grass (such as Morton & Bassett)
3 shallots, peeled and halved
2½ cups cubed peeled Yukon Gold or red potato
1 (14½-ounce) can no-salt-added diced tomatoes, undrained
1 (14-ounce) can light coconut milk
2 tablespoons fish sauce
Freshly ground pepper (optional)
Basil leaves (optional)

1. Trim fat from lamb; cut lamb into 1-inch cubes. Set aside.

2. Place basil and next 6 ingredients in a food processor; process until a paste forms. Spoon mixture into a 3½- to 4-quart electric slow cooker. Add lamb, potato, and next 3 ingredients; stir well. Cover with lid; cook on high-heat setting 1 hour. Reduce to low-heat setting, and cook 7 hours or until lamb is tender. If desired, sprinkle with pepper, and garnish with basil leaves. Yield: 6 servings (serving size: 1⅓ cups).

Diabetic Exchanges: 1 Starch, 2 Veg, 3 L Meat
Per serving: CAL 294 (31% from fat); PRO 26.9g; FAT 10.1g (sat 4.5g); CARB 23.5g; FIB 3.4g; CHOL 73mg; IRON 3.7mg; SOD 873mg; CALC 49mg

Bouillabaisse

Ladled over thick slices of French bread, this seafood stew is a favorite in Provence.

1 tablespoon hot water
1 teaspoon saffron threads
1 tablespoon olive oil
2 cups chopped onion
1½ cups chopped celery
5 garlic cloves, minced
2 (14.5-ounce) cans no-salt-added whole tomatoes, undrained and chopped
2 (8-ounce) bottles clam juice
1½ cups water
1 cup dry white wine
2 teaspoons dried thyme
1 teaspoon fennel seeds
½ teaspoon salt
2 bay leaves
1 pound little neck clams (about 18), scrubbed
1 pound mussels (about 36), scrubbed and debearded
1 pound sea scallops
½ pound large shrimp, peeled

1. Combine hot water and saffron in a small bowl; stir well, and set aside.

2. Heat oil in a large nonstick skillet over medium-high heat. Add onion, celery, and garlic; sauté 5 minutes or until tender. Place onion mixture in a 6- to 6½-quart electric slow cooker. Add saffron-water, tomatoes, and next 7 ingredients; stir well. Cover with lid; cook on low-heat setting 6 hours.

3. Increase to high-heat setting. Add clams; cover and cook 20 minutes. Add mussels, scallops, and

Curry Stew with Lamb

shrimp; cover and cook 10 to 15 minutes or until clams and mussels open (be careful not to overcook scallops and shrimp). Discard any unopened shells and bay leaves. Yield: 6 servings (serving size: 2 cups).

Diabetic Exchanges: ½ Starch, 2 Veg, 3½ V-L Meat
Per serving: CAL 243 (19% from fat); PRO 30.8g; FAT 5.1g (sat 0.8g); CARB 18.4g; FIB 3.3g; CHOL 98mg; IRON 8.9mg; SOD 768mg; CALC 146mg

Venison Chili ✓

2   pounds ground venison or ground sirloin
1   cup chopped onion
1   tablespoon Worcestershire sauce
2   teaspoons chili powder
1   (28-ounce) can whole tomatoes, undrained and coarsely chopped
1   (16-ounce) can pinto beans, drained
1   (15-ounce) can tomato sauce
1   (7-ounce) can mushroom pieces, drained
⅓   cup sliced jalapeño pepper (about 2 large peppers)
1   teaspoon ground cumin

Sliced jalapeños give a spicy kick to Venison Chili. Remove the seeds and membranes if you prefer less heat.

1. Cook venison, onion, Worcestershire sauce, and chili powder in a nonstick skillet over medium-high heat until meat is browned, stirring to crumble. Place meat mixture in a 4-quart electric slow cooker. Add tomatoes and remaining ingredients; stir well. Cover with lid; cook on high-heat setting 1 hour. Reduce to low-heat setting, and cook 3 hours. Yield: 8 servings (serving size: 1½ cups).

Diabetic Exchanges: 1 Starch, 2 Veg, 5 V-L Meat
Per serving: CAL 294 (14% from fat); PRO 40.3g; FAT 4.7g (sat 1.6g); CARB 23.6g; FIB 6.3g; CHOL 129mg; IRON 7.8mg; SOD 996mg; CALC 95mg

Caribbean Fish Pot

Acidic ingredients, such as tomatoes, can prevent potatoes from getting tender. That's why the potatoes are precooked in this recipe.

2   teaspoons vegetable oil
2   cups diced peeled red potato
1   cup chopped onion
¾   cup diced red bell pepper
⅔   cup chopped celery
4   garlic cloves, minced
2   (14.5-ounce) cans diced tomatoes with garlic and onion, undrained
2   (8-ounce) bottles clam juice
3   tablespoons pickled jalapeño pepper slices, minced
1   teaspoon dried thyme
¼   teaspoon ground allspice
¾   pound grouper or other firm white fish fillet, cut into 1-inch cubes
¾   pound large shrimp, peeled

1. Heat oil in a large nonstick skillet over medium-high heat. Add potato and next 3 ingredients; sauté 5 minutes. Add garlic; sauté 30 seconds. Cover, reduce heat to medium, and cook 5 minutes or until potato is tender. Place potato mixture in a 4½-quart electric slow cooker. Add tomatoes and next 4 ingredients; stir well. Cover with lid; cook on low-heat setting 7 hours. Add grouper and shrimp; cover and cook 45 minutes or until fish flakes easily when tested with a fork. Yield: 6 servings (serving size: 1¾ cups).

Diabetic Exchanges: 1 Starch, 2 Veg, 2 V-L Meat
Per serving: CAL 212 (15% from fat); PRO 22.3g; FAT 3.7g (sat 0.4g); CARB 24.4g; FIB 3.3g; CHOL 90mg; IRON 4.3mg; SOD 1,000mg; CALC 84mg

Meatballs with Chutney Sauce 🕐

To ensure that you get a lean product, ask the butcher to grind a lean boneless leg of lamb.

1½ pounds lean boneless leg of lamb, ground
½ cup dry breadcrumbs
¼ cup finely chopped green onions
3 tablespoons minced seeded pickled jalapeño peppers
½ teaspoon freshly ground black pepper
1 large egg
2 garlic cloves, minced
½ cup mango chutney
¼ cup no-salt-added tomato paste
3 tablespoons soy sauce
2 tablespoons pickled jalapeño pepper liquid
2 teaspoons finely chopped fresh mint
6 cups hot cooked couscous, cooked without salt or fat
1 tablespoon thinly sliced fresh mint

1. Combine ground lamb, breadcrumbs, green onions, minced jalapeño, black pepper, egg, and garlic in a bowl; stir well. Shape into 42 (1-inch) meatballs. Place meatballs in a 3½- to 4-quart electric slow cooker.

2. Combine chutney and next 4 ingredients in a bowl; stir well. Pour over meatballs. Cover with lid; cook on high-heat setting 1 hour. Reduce to low-heat setting, and cook 2 hours or until done. Serve meatballs and sauce over couscous. Sprinkle with thinly sliced mint. Yield: 6 servings (serving size: 7 meatballs, 2½ tablespoons sauce, 1 cup couscous, and ½ teaspoon mint).

Diabetic Exchanges: 4 Starch, 3 L Meat
Per serving: CAL 452 (20% from fat); PRO 32.8g; FAT 10.0g (sat 2.7g); CARB 55.8g; FIB 3.4g; CHOL 108mg; IRON 3.8mg; SOD 849mg; CALC 59mg

A cucumber-yogurt salad is a refreshing side dish for Meatballs with Chutney Sauce.

extras

Saucy Apples 'n' Pears with
light vanilla ice cream

Wild Mushroom Polenta

Saucy Apples 'n' Pears ⓥ

3   Gala apples (about 1½ pounds), peeled and sliced
3   Anjou or Bartlett pears (about 1½ pounds), peeled and sliced
1   tablespoon fresh lemon juice
½   cup firmly packed dark brown sugar
½   cup pure maple syrup
¼   cup butter or stick margarine, melted
¼   cup chopped pecans
¼   cup raisins
½   teaspoon ground cinnamon
2   tablespoons water
1   tablespoon cornstarch

1. Place apple, pear, and lemon juice in a 4½-quart electric slow cooker; toss gently.

2. Combine brown sugar, syrup, and butter; stir well. Spoon sugar mixture over fruit. Add pecans, raisins, and cinnamon; stir gently. Cover with lid; cook on low-heat setting 5½ hours.

3. Combine water and cornstarch in a small bowl; stir until well blended. Stir cornstarch mixture into fruit mixture. Cover and cook 20 minutes or until slightly thick; stir well. Serve with light vanilla ice cream or fat-free pound cake. Yield: 13 servings (serving size: ⅓ cup).

Diabetic Exchanges: 1 Starch, 1 Fruit, 1 Fat
Per serving: CAL 165 (28% from fat); PRO 0.6g; FAT 5.5g (sat 2.4g); CARB 30.9g; FIB 2.0g; CHOL 10mg; IRON 0.6mg; SOD 41mg; CALC 26mg

Wild Mushroom Polenta ⓥ

1   cup yellow cornmeal (not self-rising or cornmeal mix)
1   tablespoon butter or stick margarine
Cooking spray
3   cups boiling water
¼   cup (1 ounce) shredded fresh Parmesan cheese
2   tablespoons chopped dried porcini mushrooms
½   teaspoon salt
¼   teaspoon pepper
¼   teaspoon dried thyme
Thyme sprigs (optional)

1. Place cornmeal and butter in a 3½-quart electric slow cooker coated with cooking spray. Gradually add 3 cups boiling water, stirring constantly with a whisk until well blended. Stir in cheese and

next 4 ingredients. Cover with lid; cook on low-heat setting 3 hours or until thick. Stir well before serving. Garnish with thyme sprigs, if desired. Yield: 6 servings (serving size: ½ cup).

Diabetic Exchanges: 1 Starch, 1 Fat
Per serving: CAL 121 (29% from fat); PRO 4.4g; FAT 4.0g (sat 2.1g); CARB 17.4g; FIB 2.0g; CHOL 8mg; IRON 1.4mg; SOD 303mg; CALC 63mg

Chocolate Bread Pudding ⓥ

1   cup semisweet chocolate chips (about 8 ounces), divided
2½ cups fat-free milk
3   large egg whites
1   large egg
1   cup sugar
2   teaspoons vanilla extract
½   (16-ounce) package twin French bread loaves (1 loaf, such as Pepperidge Farm), cut into 1-inch cubes

1. Place ½ cup chocolate chips in a medium glass bowl. Microwave at HIGH 2 minutes or until chocolate melts, stirring every 30 seconds. Let cool slightly. Place milk in a 1-quart glass measure or glass bowl. Microwave at HIGH 1 minute or until warm. Gradually add milk to chocolate, stirring with a whisk until well blended. Let cool. Add egg whites and egg; stir until well blended. Stir in sugar and vanilla.

2. Place bread cubes and remaining ½ cup chocolate chips in a 3- to 4-quart electric slow cooker. Pour milk mixture over bread, tossing to moisten bread. Cover with lid, and cook on low-heat setting 4 hours or until pudding is slightly puffed and set. Yield: 8 servings (serving size: ¾ cup).

Diabetic Exchanges: 3½ Starch, ½ Sk Milk
Per serving: CAL 319 (21% from fat); PRO 8.3g; FAT 7.8g (sat 4.1g); CARB 57.2g; FIB 2.1g; CHOL 28mg; IRON 1.5mg; SOD 244mg; CALC 126mg

Bean and Salsa Dip ⓥ

1   (16-ounce) can fat-free refried beans
1   (14½-ounce) can diced tomatoes, undrained
1   (10-ounce) can diced tomatoes with green chiles, undrained
1   (4.5-ounce) can chopped green chiles, undrained

1 (4¼-ounce) can chopped ripe olives, undrained
¾ cup frozen whole-kernel corn, thawed
½ cup sliced green onions
1 teaspoon ground cumin
1 teaspoon chili powder
½ teaspoon garlic powder
¼ teaspoon ground red pepper
½ cup minced fresh cilantro
1½ cups (6 ounces) shredded reduced-fat sharp Cheddar cheese
18 ounces baked tortilla chips (such as Tostitos)

1. Place first 11 ingredients in a 4-quart electric slow cooker; stir well. Cover with lid; cook on low-heat setting 2 to 4 hours. Turn slow cooker off; stir in cilantro. Sprinkle cheese over dip; cover and let stand 5 minutes or until cheese melts (do not stir). Serve with baked tortilla chips. Yield: 18 servings (serving size: ⅓ cup dip and about 9 chips).

Diabetic Exchanges: 2 Starch, ½ Veg, ½ Fat
Per serving: CAL 187 (19% from fat); PRO 6.3g; FAT 3.9g (sat 1.5g); CARB 32.2g; FIB 4.5g; CHOL 7mg; IRON 1.3mg; SOD 562mg; CALC 130mg

The robust flavor of Cheesy Spinach-Artichoke Dip comes from three cheeses and sun-dried tomatoes.

Cheesy Spinach-Artichoke Dip

11 (6-inch) pita bread rounds
⅓ cup chopped sun-dried tomatoes, packed without oil
1 cup boiling water
1 (14-ounce) can quartered artichoke hearts, drained and coarsely chopped
1 (10-ounce) package frozen chopped spinach, thawed, drained, and squeezed dry
1 (8-ounce) tub light cream cheese, softened
1 (8-ounce) carton 30%-less-fat sour cream (such as Breakstone)
¾ cup grated Parmesan cheese
¾ cup fat-free milk
½ cup (2 ounces) crumbled reduced-fat feta cheese
½ cup diced onion
½ cup fat-free mayonnaise
1 tablespoon red wine vinegar
¼ teaspoon freshly ground pepper
2 garlic cloves, crushed

1. Preheat oven to 350°.

2. Split each pita bread in half horizontally; cut each half into 6 wedges. Place pita wedges in a single layer on baking sheets, and bake at 350° for 10 minutes or until toasted. Set aside.

3. Combine sun-dried tomatoes and boiling water in a bowl; let stand 1 hour or until soft.

4. Place artichoke and next 11 ingredients in a 3½-quart electric slow cooker; stir well. Cover with lid; cook on low-heat setting 1 hour. Drain tomatoes; stir into dip. Cover and cook 1 hour. Serve warm with toasted pita wedges. Yield: 21 servings (serving size: ¼ cup dip and about 6 pita wedges).

Diabetic Exchanges: 2½ Starch, 1 Fat
Per serving: CAL 166 (26% from fat); PRO 7.6g; FAT 4.8g (sat 2.9g); CARB 22.9g; FIB 1.3g; CHOL 14mg; IRON 1.4mg; SOD 429mg; CALC 140mg

Caramelized Onions

These tender, golden onions can be eaten as a side dish, served on hamburgers or steak, or used to make French Onion Soup, page 54.

2 extra-large sweet onions (about 3 pounds), peeled
1 (10½-ounce) can condensed beef broth, undiluted
¼ cup butter or stick margarine, cut into small pieces

1. Cut onions in half lengthwise; cut each half crosswise into ½-inch-thick slices.

2. Place onion slices, broth, and butter in a 3½-quart electric slow cooker. Cover with lid; cook on high-heat setting 8 hours or until golden, stirring after 4 hours. Store onions in an airtight container; refrigerate for up to 2 weeks, or freeze for up to 2 months. Yield: 12 servings (serving size: ¼ cup).

Diabetic Exchanges: 2 Veg, 1 Fat
Per serving: CAL 79 (45% from fat); PRO 1.6g; FAT 4.1g (sat 2.5g); CARB 9.9g; FIB 2.0g; CHOL 10mg; IRON 0.3mg; SOD 132mg; CALC 24mg

Chunky Peach-Ginger Chutney ⊘

If you use frozen peaches, there's no need to thaw them first. This chutney thickens as it stands as well as when it chills.

Cooking spray
2   cups chopped onion
4   cups fresh or frozen sliced peeled peaches
1   cup golden raisins
1   cup firmly packed light brown sugar
¼   cup chopped crystallized ginger
1   teaspoon mustard seeds
½   teaspoon ground ginger
¼   teaspoon ground cinnamon
¼   teaspoon ground cloves
¼   cup all-purpose flour
¼   cup cider vinegar

1. Coat a large nonstick skillet with cooking spray, and place over medium-high heat until hot. Add chopped onion, and sauté 5 minutes or until tender.

2. Place onion and next 8 ingredients in a 3-quart electric slow cooker; stir well. Combine flour and vinegar in a small bowl; stir with a whisk until well blended. Add flour mixture to peach mixture; stir well.

3. Cover with lid; cook on low-heat setting 5 hours. Serve chutney warm or chilled with grilled or roasted pork, chicken, or lamb. Yield: 4¼ cups (serving size: ¼ cup).

Diabetic Exchanges: 1 Starch, 1 Fruit
Per serving: CAL 113 (1% from fat); PRO 1.0g; FAT 0.2g (sat 0.0g); CARB 28.7g; FIB 1.6g; CHOL 0mg; IRON 0.7mg; SOD 7mg; CALC 26mg

Apple-Nut Muffin Cake with Brown Butter Glaze ⊘

1½ cups all-purpose flour
¾   cup firmly packed light brown sugar
½   cup graham cracker crumbs (about 3½ sheets)
2   teaspoons baking powder
1   teaspoon ground cinnamon
½   teaspoon salt
1⅓ cups finely chopped peeled Rome apple
⅓   cup chopped pecans
¾   cup 1% low-fat milk
¼   cup vegetable oil
1   large egg
Baking spray with flour
Brown Butter Glaze

1. Combine first 6 ingredients in a medium bowl; stir well. Add apple and pecans; toss gently. Make a well in center of mixture.

2. Combine milk, oil, and egg in a small bowl; stir well (do not overmix). Add to flour mixture,

Chunky Peach-Ginger Chutney turns plain grilled or roasted meats into a gourmet meal.

stirring just until moist. Spoon batter into a 6-cup miniature Bundt pan coated with baking spray. Cover pan tightly with foil.

3. Pour 2 cups hot water into crockery insert of a round 4-quart electric slow cooker. Carefully place Bundt pan in water in slow cooker. Cover slow cooker with lid; cook on high-heat setting 3½ to 4 hours or until a wooden pick inserted in center of cake comes out clean. Remove Bundt pan from slow cooker; uncover and let cool on a wire rack 10 minutes. Invert cake onto a serving plate. Let cool slightly (about 30 minutes). Pour warm Brown Butter Glaze over cake. Serve warm. Yield: 10 servings (serving size: 1 slice).

Note: If you do not have a miniature Bundt pan, you may use an 8-inch round cake pan with 3-inch-deep sides, such as a Wilton cake pan. Place a rack, trivet, or 3 canning jar rings in the bottom of the crockery insert. Place cake pan on rack, and increase hot water to 3 cups. Proceed with directions above, cooking on high-heat setting 4 hours.

Diabetic Exchanges: 3½ Starch, 2 Fat
Per serving: CAL 327 (33% from fat); PRO 4.0g; FAT 12.2g (sat 2.5g); CARB 52.2g; FIB 1.5g; CHOL 28mg; IRON 1.8mg; SOD 298mg; CALC 108mg

Brown Butter Glaze:

2   tablespoons butter or stick margarine
¼   cup firmly packed brown sugar
1   tablespoon water
¾   cup sifted powdered sugar
2   teaspoons water
¼   teaspoon vanilla extract

1. Melt butter in a small saucepan over medium heat. Cook 2 minutes or just until butter turns light brown, stirring constantly (be careful not to burn butter). Remove from heat, and let cool slightly. Add brown sugar and 1 tablespoon water; return to medium heat, and cook 30 seconds or until sugar dissolves, stirring constantly.

2. Remove from heat. Add powdered sugar, stirring until smooth. Stir in 2 teaspoons water and vanilla. Yield: ½ cup.

Hot Chocolate ⊙

⅓   cup unsweetened cocoa
5½   cups fat-free milk, divided
1   tablespoon vanilla extract
1   (14-ounce) can fat-free sweetened condensed milk
1   (3-inch) cinnamon stick (optional)
30   miniature marshmallows

1. Place cocoa in a 3-quart electric slow cooker. Gradually add 1 cup fat-free milk, stirring with a whisk until well blended. Add remaining fat-free milk, vanilla, and sweetened condensed milk, stirring with a whisk until well blended. Add cinnamon stick, if desired. Cover with lid; cook on low-heat setting 4 to 8 hours. Discard cinnamon stick. Stir well with a whisk before serving. Ladle hot chocolate into mugs; top with marshmallows. Yield: 10 servings (serving size: ¾ cup hot chocolate and 3 marshmallows).

Diabetic Exchanges: 2 Starch, ½ Sk Milk
Per serving: CAL 177 (2% from fat); PRO 9.1g; FAT 0.5g (sat 0.2g); CARB 34.5g; FIB 1.0g; CHOL 5mg; IRON 0.4mg; SOD 115mg; CALC 280mg

Sweet-and-Sour Baked Beans ⊙

Cooking spray
2   cups chopped onion
3   (16-ounce) cans light red kidney beans, rinsed and drained
6   bacon slices, cooked and crumbled
¾   cup ketchup
⅓   cup firmly packed brown sugar
⅓   cup pure maple syrup
¼   cup cider vinegar
¼   cup water
1   tablespoon dry mustard

1. Coat a large nonstick skillet with cooking spray; place over medium-high heat until hot. Add onion; sauté 3 minutes or until tender.

2. Place onion and remaining ingredients in a 3½- to 4-quart electric slow cooker; stir well. Cover with lid; cook on low-heat setting 6 hours. Yield: 10 servings (serving size: ½ cup).

Diabetic Exchanges: 2½ Starch
Per serving: CAL 205 (9% from fat); PRO 8.0g; FAT 2.2g (sat 0.5g); CARB 40.2g; FIB 8.0g; CHOL 4mg; IRON 0.6mg; SOD 299mg; CALC 26mg

Hot Chocolate

Salsa Cheesecake

Served with baked tortilla chips, this appetizer will be a hit at your next party.

Cooking spray
1 tablespoon dry breadcrumbs
1 (8-ounce) tub chive and onion light cream cheese, softened
1 (8-ounce) tub light cream cheese, softened
½ cup medium salsa
1 (4.5-ounce) can chopped green chiles, undrained
1 tablespoon all-purpose flour
1 teaspoon chili powder
1 large egg
1 large egg white
½ cup (2 ounces) shredded reduced-fat Mexican cheese blend (such as Sargento)
¼ cup sliced ripe olives
¼ cup chopped red bell pepper
3 tablespoons sliced green onions
3 tablespoons frozen whole-kernel corn, thawed

1. Coat a 7-inch springform pan with cooking spray; sprinkle breadcrumbs over bottom of pan.

2. Beat cream cheeses at medium speed of a mixer until smooth. Add salsa, green chiles, flour, and chili powder; beat just until blended. Add egg and egg white; beat just until blended (do not overbeat or cheesecake will crack). Stir in Mexican cheese. Pour cheese mixture into prepared pan.

3. Place a 10-ounce custard cup or ramekin, upside down, in crockery insert of a round 4-quart electric slow cooker. Place springform pan on top of custard cup. Carefully pour 3 cups hot water around the sides of the springform pan. Cover with lid; cook on high-heat setting 1 hour and 45 minutes or until cheesecake is set.

4. Turn slow cooker off. Uncover; gently remove moisture from top of cheesecake with paper towel (do not remove pan from crockery insert). Carefully run a knife around edge of cheesecake. Remove crockery insert from slow cooker. Let cheesecake stand in crockery insert, uncovered, 30 minutes.

5. Remove pan from crockery insert, and let cheesecake cool completely in pan on a wire rack. Cover and chill 8 to 24 hours.

6. Carefully remove sides from springform pan. Beginning at outside edge of cheesecake, arrange olives, bell pepper, and green onions in concentric circles on top of cheesecake, ending with corn in center of cheesecake. Cut into wedges. Yield: 12 servings (serving size: 1 wedge).

Diabetic Exchanges: ½ Starch, 1 M-F Meat, ½ Fat
Per serving: CAL 115 (56% from fat); PRO 6.8g; FAT 7.3g (sat 4.6g); CARB 6.0g; FIB 1.2g; CHOL 37mg; IRON 0.5mg; SOD 357mg; CALC 99mg

Old-Fashioned Apple Butter

5 Gala apples or other baking apples (about 2 pounds), peeled and sliced
½ cup sugar
½ cup firmly packed brown sugar
½ teaspoon ground cinnamon

1. Place all ingredients in a 4½-quart electric slow cooker; stir well.

2. Cover with lid; cook on high-heat setting 1 hour. Reduce to low-heat setting, and cook 8 to 9 hours or until apples are very tender. Stir with a whisk to break up any large pieces. Store apple butter in refrigerator for up to 1 week. Serve with breakfast breads. Yield: 2½ cups (serving size: 2 tablespoons).

Diabetic Exchanges: 1 Starch
Per serving: CAL 66 (2% from fat); PRO 0.1g; FAT 0.1g (sat 0.0g); CARB 17.1g; FIB 0.9g; CHOL 0mg; IRON 0.1mg; SOD 2mg; CALC 7mg

Harvest Steamed Pudding with Orange-Pecan Sauce ☺

For best results, bake a large sweet potato, then peel and mash it. Steamed puddings have a firm texture and slice much like a cake.

Cooking spray
1   cup firmly packed light brown sugar
¼   cup butter or stick margarine, softened
1   large egg
3   large egg whites
¾   cup mashed cooked sweet potato
½   cup 1% low-fat milk
2¼ cups all-purpose flour
1½ teaspoons baking powder
½   teaspoon baking soda
½   teaspoon salt
½   teaspoon ground cinnamon
¼   teaspoon ground nutmeg
½   cup raisins
Orange-Pecan Sauce

1. Coat a 6-cup steamed pudding mold and lid with cooking spray. Set aside.

2. Combine brown sugar and butter in a large bowl; beat at medium speed of a mixer until well blended (about 5 minutes). Add egg and egg whites, 1 at a time, beating well after each addition.

3. Combine sweet potato and milk in a bowl; stir well, and set aside. Combine flour, baking powder, baking soda, salt, cinnamon, and nutmeg in a bowl; stir well. Add flour mixture to sugar mixture alternately with sweet potato mixture, beginning and ending with flour mixture. Stir in raisins.

4. Spoon batter into prepared mold; cover with lid. Place mold in crockery insert of a round 4½-quart electric slow cooker. Cover slow cooker with lid; cook on high-heat setting 4 hours or until a wooden pick inserted in center of steamed pudding comes out clean.

5. Remove mold from slow cooker; uncover and let cool on a wire rack 15 minutes. Invert pudding onto rack. Let cool slightly. Serve warm or at room temperature with Orange-Pecan Sauce. Yield: 12 servings (serving size: 1 slice and about 1 tablespoon sauce).

Note: To prepare steamed pudding in a coffee can, prepare batter as directed above. Spoon batter into a (1-pound, 10-ounce) coffee can. Cover can with foil. Proceed with directions at left, using a 3½- to 4-quart electric slow cooker. Cook on high-heat setting 5 hours.

Diabetic Exchanges: 3½ Starch, 1½ Fat
Per serving: CAL 310 (23% from fat); PRO 5.9g; FAT 8.1g (sat 4.0g); CARB 54.6g; FIB 1.6g; CHOL 33mg; IRON 2.1mg; SOD 349mg; CALC 96mg

Orange-Pecan Sauce:

½   cup tub-style light cream cheese, softened
¼   cup firmly packed light brown sugar
¼   cup chopped pecans, toasted
3½ tablespoons orange marmalade

1. Beat cream cheese at low speed of a mixer until smooth. Add brown sugar, and beat well. Stir in pecans and orange marmalade. Cover and chill. Yield: about 1 cup (serving size: about 1 tablespoon).

Mashed sweet potatoes lend a moist, tender crumb to Harvest Steamed Pudding with Orange-Pecan Sauce.

Caramel Pie

Caramel Pie

1 (14-ounce) can fat-free sweetened
   condensed milk
1 (6-ounce) package reduced-fat graham
   cracker crust
1 (8-ounce) container frozen reduced-calorie
   whipped topping, thawed
1 (1.4-ounce) milk chocolate-crisp butter
   toffee candy bar (such as Skor), coarsely
   chopped

1. Pour milk into a 2-cup glass measure; cover with foil. Place in a 3- to 4-quart electric slow cooker. Add very hot water to slow cooker to reach level of milk in measure. Cover slow cooker with lid; cook on low-heat setting 9 hours (milk should be the color of caramel).

2. Pour caramelized milk into crust; let cool. Spread whipped topping over pie, and sprinkle with chopped candy bar. Yield: 8 servings.

Diabetic Exchanges: 3½ Starch, 1½ Fat
Per serving: CAL 327 (25% from fat); PRO 5.6g; FAT 8.8g (sat 5.1g); CARB 53.9g; FIB 0.1g; CHOL 6mg; IRON 0.4mg; SOD 151mg; CALC 146mg

Hash Brown Potato Casserole ⏱

1 (26-ounce) package frozen shredded hash
   brown potatoes
1 (10¾-ounce) can condensed reduced-fat,
   reduced-sodium cream of mushroom or
   cream of chicken soup, undiluted
1⅓ cups fat-free milk
¼ cup finely chopped onion
1 tablespoon butter or stick margarine, cut
   into small pieces
¾ teaspoon pepper
½ teaspoon salt
Cooking spray
1 cup (4 ounces) shredded Cheddar cheese

1. Place first 7 ingredients in a 5-quart electric slow cooker coated with cooking spray; stir well. Cover with lid; cook on high-heat setting 1 hour. Reduce to low-heat setting, and cook 4 to 5 hours. Add cheese, stirring gently. Cover and cook 30 minutes. Yield: 8 servings (serving size: ¾ cup).

Diabetic Exchanges: 1½ Starch, 1 Fat
Per serving: CAL 163 (38% from fat); PRO 6.5g; FAT 6.9g (sat 4.2g); CARB 19.0g; FIB 1.2g; CHOL 23mg; IRON 0.5mg; SOD 428mg; CALC 185mg

Cranberry-Cardamom Relish

1½ cups sugar
1 (2-inch) piece vanilla bean, split
1 (12-ounce) bag fresh or frozen cranberries
1½ tablespoons orange zest
2 tablespoons fresh orange juice
1 teaspoon ground cardamom

1. Place sugar in a 3-quart electric slow cooker. Scrape seeds from vanilla bean; add seeds and bean to sugar. Add cranberries and remaining ingredients to sugar; stir well. Cover with lid; cook on low-heat setting 8 hours.

2. Mash cranberries slightly with back of a spoon. Discard vanilla bean. Serve relish warm or chilled. Yield: 2 cups (serving size: 2 tablespoons).

Diabetic Exchanges: 1½ Starch
Per serving: CAL 85 (1% from fat); PRO 0.1g; FAT 0.1g (sat 0.0g); CARB 21.9g; FIB 1.0g; CHOL 0mg; IRON 0.1mg; SOD 0mg; CALC 3mg

Citrus Wassail

12 whole cloves
3   (3-inch) cinnamon sticks
1   (750-milliliter) bottle Cabernet Sauvignon
    or other dry red wine
1   (64-ounce) bottle cranberry-tangerine
    juice drink
2   (12-ounce) cans frozen citrus beverage
    concentrate (such as Five Alive), thawed
    and undiluted
½   cup water

1. Place cloves and cinnamon sticks on a 6-inch square of cheesecloth; tie ends of cheesecloth securely.

2. Place spice bag, wine, and remaining ingredients in a 4- to 6-quart electric slow cooker; stir well. Cover with lid; cook on low-heat setting 7 hours. Discard spice bag. Serve beverage warm or chilled. Yield: 13 servings (serving size: 1 cup).

Note: For a nonalcoholic beverage, replace the wine with 3¼ cups purple grape juice and increase the cloves to 40.

Diabetic Exchanges: 2 Starch, 1 Fruit
Per serving: CAL 175 (0% from fat); PRO 0.1g; FAT 0.0g (sat 0.0g); CARB 46.2g; FIB 0.0g; CHOL 0mg; IRON 0.2mg; SOD 25mg; CALC 4mg

Vanilla Bean Rice Pudding ⏱

6   cups 2% reduced-fat milk
1½ cups uncooked converted rice (such as Uncle Ben's)
1   cup sugar
1   cup raisins
3   tablespoons butter or stick margarine, melted
½   teaspoon salt
1   vanilla bean, split
1   large egg
½   teaspoon ground cinnamon
1   (8-ounce) carton 30%-less-fat sour cream (such as Breakstone)

1. Place first 6 ingredients in a 3½- to 4-quart electric slow cooker; stir well. Scrape seeds from vanilla bean; add seeds and bean to milk mixture. Cover with lid; cook on high-heat setting 2½ to 4 hours or until rice is tender and most of liquid is absorbed (do not overcook).

2. Place egg in a small bowl; stir well with a whisk. Gradually add ½ cup hot rice mixture to egg, stirring constantly with whisk. Return egg mixture to slow cooker, stirring constantly with whisk. Cook 1 minute, stirring constantly. Turn slow cooker off; let stand 5 minutes. Stir in ½ teaspoon cinnamon and sour cream. Discard vanilla bean. Serve warm. Yield: 12 servings (serving size: ¾ cup).

Diabetic Exchanges: 3 Starch, ½ Fruit, 1 Fat
Per serving: CAL 317 (23% from fat); PRO 7.8g; FAT 8.2g (sat 4.9g); CARB 53.9g; FIB 0.9g; CHOL 44mg; IRON 1.3mg; SOD 208mg; CALC 205mg

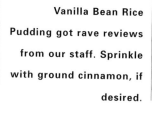

Vanilla Bean Rice Pudding got rave reviews from our staff. Sprinkle with ground cinnamon, if desired.

Fudgy Caramel Pudding Cake ⏱

Be sure to scoop the warm caramel sauce from the bottom of the dish when serving this gooey dessert.

1   (19.8-ounce) box fudge brownie mix (such as Betty Crocker)
1   cup water
½   cup unsweetened applesauce
3   tablespoons vegetable oil
1   large egg
1   large egg white
Cooking spray
½   cup fat-free caramel-flavored sundae syrup
2   tablespoons chopped walnuts or pecans
2¾ cups vanilla fat-free frozen yogurt

1. Combine first 5 ingredients in a large bowl; stir with a wooden spoon 50 strokes. Set aside.

2. Beat egg white with clean, dry beaters at high speed of a mixer until stiff peaks form. Gently fold egg white into batter. Pour batter into a 2-quart soufflé dish or deep-sided round baking dish coated with cooking spray. Drizzle caramel syrup over batter; sprinkle with nuts (caramel will sink to bottom).

3. Place a long sheet of foil over top of dish and wrap edges under dish. Place dish on top of another long sheet of foil; press foil against sides and over top of dish, completely enclosing dish. Place a small rack, trivet, or 3 canning jar rings in crockery insert of a round 5-quart electric slow cooker; pour 3 cups water into bottom of slow cooker. Place dish on rack in water. Cover slow cooker with lid; cook on high-heat setting 4½ hours or until pudding is set. Remove foil, and let stand 20

minutes. Spoon into bowls; top with frozen yogurt. Yield: 11 servings (serving size: ½ cup pudding cake and ¼ cup frozen yogurt).

Diabetic Exchanges: 4 Starch, 2 Fat
Per serving: CAL 357 (26% from fat); PRO 5.8g; FAT 10.7g (sat 1.9g); CARB 61.3g; FIB 1.6g; CHOL 22mg; IRON 2.2mg; SOD 274mg; CALC 61mg

German Potato Salad ⏱

Some prep time is required to get this dish simmering, but then no supervision is required. Buy precooked bacon to save time.

4½ pounds medium red potatoes (about 15)
4 medium onions, thinly sliced (about 5 cups)
⅔ cup all-purpose flour
⅔ cup sugar
1 tablespoon salt
5 teaspoons dry mustard
2½ teaspoons celery seeds
1¼ teaspoons pepper
1⅓ cups water
1 cup cider vinegar
4 bacon slices, cooked and crumbled
2 hard-cooked large eggs, peeled and chopped

1. Place potatoes in a large Dutch oven; cover with water. Bring to a boil, and cook 20 minutes or until tender. Let cool slightly. Cut potatoes into quarters.

2. Place sliced onion in a 4-quart electric slow cooker; top with potatoes.

3. Combine flour and next 5 ingredients in a large saucepan; gradually add water and vinegar, stirring with a whisk until well blended. Place over medium-high heat, and cook until slightly thick, stirring constantly. Pour over vegetables in slow cooker.

4. Cover with lid; cook on high-heat setting 1 hour. Reduce to low-heat setting, and cook 4 hours. Sprinkle with crumbled bacon, and top with egg. Serve warm. Yield: 16 servings (serving size: ¾ cup).

Diabetic Exchanges: 2½ Starch, 1 Veg
Per serving: CAL 204 (9% from fat); PRO 4.9g; FAT 2.0g (sat 0.5g); CARB 42.9g; FIB 3.4g; CHOL 25mg; IRON 2.2mg; SOD 479mg; CALC 32mg

German Potato Salad slow cooks in a sweet-tart vinaigrette before it's served warm with crumbled bacon and chopped egg.

Candy Bar Cheesecake

⅔   cup chocolate graham cracker crumbs (about 4 cookie sheets)
Cooking spray
1   cup fat-free cottage cheese
2   (8-ounce) tubs light cream cheese, softened
¾   cup firmly packed brown sugar
½   cup sugar
½   cup fat-free sour cream
¼   cup all-purpose flour
2   teaspoons vanilla extract
2   large eggs
2   large egg whites
¼   cup fat-free caramel-flavored sundae syrup, divided
2   (2.07-ounce) chocolate-coated caramel-peanut nougat bars (such as Snickers), chopped and divided

1. Sprinkle crumbs into bottom of an 8-inch springform pan coated with cooking spray.

2. Place cheeses in a food processor; process 1 minute or until smooth. Add brown sugar and next 4 ingredients; process just until blended, stopping once to scrape down sides. With processor on, add eggs and egg whites through food chute, processing just until blended (do not over-process or cheesecake will crack).

3. Pour half of batter into prepared pan. Drizzle with 2 tablespoons syrup, and sprinkle with half of chopped candy bars. Pour remaining batter into pan.

4. Place 3 (6-ounce) custard cups, upside-down, in crockery insert of an oval 6-quart electric slow cooker. Place springform pan on top of custard cups. Carefully pour 3 cups hot water around the sides of the springform pan. Cover with lid; cook on high-heat setting 3 hours or until cheesecake is set.

5. Turn slow cooker off. Remove pan from slow cooker, and place on a wire rack. Remove any excess moisture from top of cheesecake with a paper towel. Carefully run a sharp knife around edge of cheesecake. Let cheesecake cool completely in pan on a wire rack.

Red Cabbage and Apples pair perfectly with grilled low-fat sausages or roasted pork.

Red Cabbage and Apples ⊙

Add color and vitamins to this dish by leaving the peel on the apples.

2   bacon slices
1¼ cups chopped red onion
8   cups thinly sliced red cabbage
3   cups diced Granny Smith apple
3   tablespoons brown sugar
3   tablespoons balsamic vinegar
½   teaspoon salt
⅛   teaspoon pepper

1. Cook bacon in a large skillet over medium-high heat until crisp; remove bacon from skillet. Cover and chill. Reserve bacon drippings in skillet. Add onion to drippings; sauté over medium-high heat 3 minutes or until lightly browned.

2. Place onion in a 4-quart electric slow cooker. Add cabbage and next 5 ingredients; stir well. Cover with lid; cook on high-heat setting 3 hours or until tender. Crumble bacon, and sprinkle over each serving. Yield: 6 servings (serving size: 1 cup cabbage mixture and 1½ teaspoons bacon).

Diabetic Exchanges: ½ Starch, 2 Veg, ½ Fruit
Per serving: CAL 111 (9% from fat); PRO 2.5g; FAT 1.3g (sat 0.4g); CARB 24.9g; FIB 4.0g; CHOL 2mg; IRON 0.9mg; SOD 252mg; CALC 67mg

6. Cover and chill 8 to 24 hours. Carefully remove sides from springform pan; drizzle cheesecake with remaining syrup, and sprinkle with remaining chopped candy. Yield: 10 servings.

Diabetic Exchanges: 4 Starch, 2 Fat
Per serving: CAL 359 (30% from fat); PRO 11.2g; FAT 11.7g (sat 6.4g); CARB 50.3g; FIB 0.6g; CHOL 67mg; IRON 1.0mg; SOD 418mg; CALC 105mg

Ratatouille

1 (1-pound) eggplant, peeled and cut into 1-inch chunks (about 3 cups)
1½ teaspoons salt, divided
1 large onion, cut in half lengthwise and sliced (about 2½ cups)
1 large green bell pepper, cut into strips (about 1½ cups)
1 large red bell pepper, cut into strips (about 1½ cups)
3 medium zucchini, sliced (about 4 cups)
2 pounds plum tomatoes, cut into ½-inch wedges
3 tablespoons tomato paste
2 tablespoons extra-virgin olive oil
¼ teaspoon black pepper
3 garlic cloves, minced
½ cup chopped fresh basil
¼ cup capers

1. Place eggplant in a colander over a sink. Sprinkle ¼ teaspoon salt over eggplant; toss well. Let stand 30 minutes to drain. Pat dry with paper towels.

2. Layer half each of onion, eggplant, bell pepper strips, zucchini, and tomatoes in a 6-quart electric slow cooker. Combine remaining 1¼ teaspoons salt, tomato paste, olive oil, black pepper, and garlic in a small bowl; stir well. Spoon half of oil mixture over vegetable mixture. Repeat layering of vegetables, ending with oil mixture.

3. Cover with lid; cook on low-heat setting 6 hours or until vegetables are tender. Stir in chopped basil and capers. Serve hot, at room temperature, or chilled. Yield: 10 servings (serving size: 1 cup).

Diabetic Exchanges: 3 Veg, ½ Fat
Per serving: CAL 83 (33% from fat); PRO 2.6g; FAT 3.4g (sat 0.5g); CARB 12.8g; FIB 3.5g; CHOL 0mg; IRON 1.1mg; SOD 466mg; CALC 28mg

Apple Grunt

This old-fashioned fruit dessert is topped with slightly sweet biscuit dough and then stewed.

5 medium Golden Delicious apples (about 2 pounds), peeled and cut into ½-inch wedges
½ cup sugar
⅓ cup all-purpose flour
¼ teaspoon apple pie spice
2 cups reduced-fat biscuit and baking mix (such as Bisquick)
¾ cup fat-free milk
3 tablespoons sugar
3 tablespoons butter or stick margarine, melted
3 cups vanilla low-fat frozen yogurt

1. Place apples, ½ cup sugar, flour, and apple pie spice in a 4-quart electric slow cooker; stir well.

2. Combine biscuit mix, milk, 3 tablespoons sugar, and butter in a bowl; stir just until moist. Spoon dough over apple mixture.

Popular in the French region of Provence, Ratatouille can be served as a side dish or as an appetizer with bread or crackers.

3. Cover with lid; cook on low-heat setting 6 hours. Divide mixture evenly between 9 dessert dishes; top each serving with ⅓ cup frozen yogurt. Serve warm. Yield: 9 servings.

Diabetic Exchanges: 3½ Starch, 1 Fruit, 1 Fat
Per serving: CAL 336 (15% from fat); PRO 5.4g; FAT 5.8g (sat 2.8g); CARB 66.5g; FIB 2.2g; CHOL 13mg; IRON 1.3mg; SOD 393mg; CALC 125mg

Lemon-Fig Preserves

2   (8-ounce) packages Calimyrna figs, coarsely chopped
1½ cups sugar
1¾ cups water
2   tablespoons lemon zest
¼   cup fresh lemon juice

1. Place all ingredients in a 3½-quart electric slow cooker; stir well. Cover with lid; cook on low-heat setting 6 hours. Spoon half of preserves into a food processor; process to desired consistency. Spoon into a bowl. Repeat procedure with remaining preserves. Spoon preserves into airtight containers, and chill 8 to 24 hours. Store preserves in refrigerator. Yield: 4 cups (serving size: 1 tablespoon).

Diabetic Exchanges: ½ Starch
Per serving: CAL 38 (1% from fat); PRO 0.2g; FAT 0.0g (sat 0.0g); CARB 9.5g; FIB 0.9g; CHOL 0mg; IRON 0.2mg; SOD 1mg; CALC 10mg

Packaged in decorative jars, Lemon-Fig Preserves are ideal for gift giving.

Root Vegetable Medley

This dish is an easy, oven-free way of preparing a side dish for Thanksgiving.

1   pound small red potatoes, cut into ½-inch wedges
1   pound turnips, peeled and cut into ½-inch cubes
1   pound sweet potatoes, peeled and cut into ½-inch cubes
½   pound celeriac, peeled and cut into ½-inch cubes
½   pound peeled baby carrots
2   cups thinly sliced fennel bulb
3   tablespoons extra-virgin olive oil
2   tablespoons balsamic vinegar
1   teaspoon salt
1   teaspoon pepper
1   teaspoon fennel seeds

1. Place all ingredients in a 6-quart electric slow cooker; toss well. Cover with lid; cook on low-heat setting 7 to 8 hours or until vegetables are tender. Yield: 8 servings (serving size: 1 cup).

Diabetic Exchanges: 2 Starch, 1 Veg, 1 Fat
Per serving: CAL 201 (25% from fat); PRO 3.4g; FAT 5.8g (sat 0.8g); CARB 35.2g; FIB 4.9g; CHOL 0mg; IRON 1.8mg; SOD 386mg; CALC 66mg

Coconut-Pecan Sweet Potatoes ⊘

2   pounds sweet potatoes, peeled and cut into 1-inch pieces (about 5½ cups)
¼   cup firmly packed brown sugar
2   tablespoons flaked sweetened coconut
2   tablespoons chopped pecans, toasted
1   tablespoon butter or stick margarine, melted
1   teaspoon vanilla extract
¼   teaspoon ground cinnamon
Cooking spray
½   cup miniature marshmallows

1. Place first 7 ingredients in a 3½-quart electric slow cooker coated with cooking spray; toss well. Cover with lid; cook on low-heat setting 6 to 8 hours or until potatoes are tender.

2. Turn slow cooker off. Sprinkle marshmallows over potatoes; cover and let stand 5 minutes. Yield: 7 servings (serving size: ½ cup).

Diabetic Exchanges: 3 Starch, ½ Fat
Per serving: CAL 208 (17% from fat); PRO 2.3g; FAT 4.1g (sat 1.8g); CARB 41.2g; FIB 2.5g; CHOL 4mg; IRON 0.9mg; SOD 42mg; CALC 35mg

There are a number of slow cookers on the market. We used five different brands in our test kitchens to test the recipes in this book. The names of the manufacturers are listed below:

1 **Hamilton Beach/Proctor-Silex, Inc.**
234 Springs Road
Washington, NC 27889
1-800-851-8900 USA
1-800-267-2826 Canada
www.hamiltonbeach.com

2 **Toastmaster Slow Cooker**
Salton/Maxim Housewares
1801 North Stadium Boulevard
Columbia, MO 65202
1-800-947-3744
www.toastmaster.com
consumer_relations@toastmaster.com

3 **The West Bend Company**
400 West Washington Street
West Bend, WI 53095-2582
(262) 334-6949
www.westbend.com

4 **The Rival Company**
c/o The Holmes Group
P.O. Box 769
Milford, MA 01757
1-800-557-4825
www.crockpot.com
service@theholmesgroup.com

5 **Deni Combo Cooker**
Keystone Manufacturing Company, Inc.
P.O. Box 863
Buffalo, NY 14240
1-800-336-4822
www.deni.com/9100.html
custserv@deni.com

S L O W   C O O K E R   Q & A

Q: Is it safe to leave a slow cooker unattended?

A: Yes. Because they operate at a low wattage, it's safe to fill them, plug them in, and let them cook for you.

Q: To save time in the morning, can I assemble the recipe in the insert and place it in the refrigerator the night before I want to cook?

A: Most recipes will work fine when prepared and refrigerated overnight. The chilled insert can go directly from the refrigerator to the heating base. However, you may find that the recipe requires extra cooking time because of the chilled ingredients and cold insert.

Q: Why are vegetables such as potatoes, carrots, and turnips sometimes not tender at the end of a recipe's cooking time?

A: Some vegetables, especially root vegetables, take longer to cook in slow cookers. Place these vegetables near the bottom and sides where they will be covered with liquid. Always layer the ingredients in the slow cooker in the order specified in the recipe.

Q: Is it necessary to brown meat before cooking it in the slow cooker?

A: Not always, but browning often helps the flavor and appearance of prepared dishes. You will find this step added to some of our recipes where we felt it improved the final product.

Q: Should I open the lid and stir the ingredients during cooking?

A: Stirring is not necessary in most recipes. You lose valuable heat when the lid is removed, which slows the cooking process.

GUIDE TO FOOD STORAGE

IN THE FREEZER
(at -10° to 0°)

Dairy

Cheese, hard	3 months
Cheese, soft	2 weeks
Egg substitute	6 months
Egg whites	6 months
Egg yolks	8 months
Ice cream, sherbet	1 month

Fruits and Vegetables

Commercially frozen fruits	1 year
Commercially frozen vegetables	8 to 12 months

Meats, Poultry, and Seafood

Beef, Lamb, and Veal

Ground, uncooked, and all cuts, cooked	3 months
Roasts and steaks, uncooked	9 months

Pork

Ground, uncooked, and all cuts, cooked	3 months
Roasts and chops, uncooked	6 months

Poultry

All cuts, cooked	1 month
Boned or bone-in pieces, uncooked	6 months

Seafood

Perch, trout, and shellfish	3 months
Cod, flounder, and halibut	6 months

IN THE REFRIGERATOR
(at 34° to 40°)

Dairy

Butter and margarine	1 month
Buttermilk, low-fat	1 to 2 weeks
Cheese, grated Parmesan	1 year
Cheeses, Cheddar and Swiss	3 to 4 weeks
Cream cheese, ⅓-less-fat, light, and fat-free	2 weeks
Eggs and egg substitute	1 month

Meats, Poultry, and Seafood

Beef, Lamb, Pork, and Veal

Ground and stew meat, uncooked	1 to 2 days
Roasts, uncooked	2 to 4 days
Steaks and chops, uncooked	3 to 5 days

Chicken, Turkey, and Seafood

All cuts, uncooked	1 to 2 days

Fruits and Vegetables

Apples, beets, cabbage, carrots, celery, citrus fruits, and parsnips	2 to 3 weeks
Apricots, berries, peaches, pears, plums, asparagus, cauliflower, cucumbers, mushrooms, okra, peas, peppers, salad greens, and summer squash	2 to 4 days
Corn, husked	1 day

IN THE PANTRY

Keep these at room temperature for six to 12 months.

Baking and Cooking Supplies

Baking powder
Biscuit and baking mix
Broth, canned
Cooking spray
Honey
Mayonnaise, light, low-fat, and fat-free (unopened)
Milk, canned evaporated fat-free
Milk, fat-free dry
Mustard, prepared (unopened)
Oils, olive and vegetable
Pasta, dried
Peanut butter, regular and reduced-fat
Rice, instant and regular
Salad dressings, bottled (unopened)
Seasoning sauces, bottled
Tuna, canned

Fruits, Legumes, and Vegetables

Fruits, canned
Legumes (beans, lentils, peas), dried or canned
Tomato products, canned
Vegetables, canned

EQUIVALENT MEASURES

3	teaspoons	1	tablespoon
4	tablespoons	¼	cup
5⅓	tablespoons	⅓	cup
8	tablespoons	½	cup
16	tablespoons	1	cup
2	tablespoons (liquid)	1	ounce
1	cup	8	fluid ounces

2	cups	1	pint (16 fluid ounces)
4	cups	1	quart
4	quarts	1	gallon
⅛	cup	2	tablespoons
⅓	cup	5	tablespoons plus 1 teaspoon
⅔	cup	10	tablespoons plus 2 teaspoons
¾	cup	12	tablespoons

FOOD	WEIGHT (OR COUNT)	YIELD
Apples	1 pound (3 medium)	3 cups sliced
Bananas	1 pound (3 medium)	2½ cups sliced or about 2 cups mashed
Bread	1 pound	12 to 16 slices
	About 1½ slices	1 cup fresh breadcrumbs
Cabbage	1 pound head	4½ cups shredded
Carrots	1 pound	3 cups shredded
Cheese, American or Cheddar	1 pound	About 4 cups shredded
cottage	1 pound	2 cups
cream	3- ounce package	6 tablespoons
Chocolate chips	6- ounce package	1 cup
Coconut, flaked or shredded	1 pound	5 cups
Coffee	1 pound	80 tablespoons (40 cups perked)
Corn	2 medium ears	1 cup kernels
Cornmeal	1 pound	3 cups
Crab, in shell	1 pound	¾ to 1 cup flaked
Dates, pitted	1 pound	3 cups chopped
	8- ounce package	1½ cups chopped
Eggs	4 large	1 cup
whites	8 to 11	1 cup
yolks	12 to 14	1 cup
Green bell pepper	1 large	1 cup diced
Lemon	1 medium	2 to 3 tablespoons juice; 2 teaspoons grated rind
Lettuce	1- pound head	6¼ cups torn
Lime	1 medium	1½ to 2 tablespoons juice; 1½ teaspoons grated rind
Macaroni	4 ounces dry (1 cup)	2 cups cooked
Margarine	1 pound	2 cups
	¼- pound stick	½ cup
Mushrooms	3 cups raw (8 ounces)	1 cup sliced cooked
Oats, quick-cooking	1 cup	1¾ cups cooked
Onion	1 medium	½ cup chopped
Orange	1 medium	½ cup juice; 2 tablespoons grated rind
Pears	2 medium	1 cup sliced
Potatoes, baking	3 medium	2 cups cubed cooked or 1¾ cups mashed
sweet	3 medium	3 cups sliced
Raisins	1 pound	3 cups
Rice, long-grain	1 cup	3 to 4 cups cooked
quick-cooking	1 cup	2 cups cooked
Shrimp, raw in shell	1½ pounds	2 cups (¾ pound) cleaned, cooked
Spaghetti	7 ounces	About 4 cups cooked
Sugar, brown	1 pound	2⅓ cups firmly packed
powdered	1 pound	3½ cups unsifted
granulated	1 pound	2 cups